P9-DBO-194

my secret is . . .
"Drink lots of water to loosen up your throat."
—NELLY

my secret is . . .
"Learn to sing from the heart."
—CHRISTINA AGUILERA

my secret is . . .
"To learn how to breathe . . . lay down on your
back." **—LUTHER VANDROSS**

my secret is . . .
"No chocolate before singing!" **—CHER**

my secret is . . .
"Concentrate on being the next *you*—not someone else!" **—BRIAN McKNIGHT**

Check out what the
STARS
have to tell you. . . .

SING LIKE THE STARS!

by ROGER LOVE

Pocket Books

New York London Toronto Sydney

POCKET BOOKS, a division of Simon & Schuster, Inc.
1230 Avenue of the Americas, New York, NY 10020

Copyright © 2003 by Roger Love

MTV Music Television and all related titles, logos, and characters are trademarks of
MTV Networks, a division of Viacom International Inc.

All rights reserved, including the right to reproduce this book or portions thereof
in any form whatsoever. For information address Pocket Books, 1230 Avenue
of the Americas, New York, NY 10020

ISBN: 0-7434-8499-1

First MTV Books/Pocket Books trade paperback edition October 2003

10 9 8 7 6 5 4

POCKET and colophon are registered trademarks of Simon & Schuster, Inc.

Cover Design
Design direction: Deklah Polansky and Christopher Truch
Design: Christopher Truch
Photography: Terry Doyle
Project management: Sarah James

Book design: Lili Schwartz

Manufactured in the United States of America

For information regarding special discounts for bulk purchases, please contact
Simon & Schuster Special Sales at 1-800-456-6798 or business@simonandschuster.com

This book is dedicated to
the "loves" in my life:
Miyoko, Madison, and Colin
and
to the memory of my mother, Sylvia,
who now sings to me from a higher place

table of
CONTENTS

YOU *CAN* SING!

chapter ONE

Millions of people around the world love to sing. With the incredible success of TV shows like *American Idol,* suddenly everything in the universe is about singing or watching other people sing. Thousands of hopefuls stood in line for days on end just to have the chance to audition to be on that show. All of those young people had one thing in common: a dream to be a great singer. To someday stand on a stage and sing their hearts out to an audience of fans that love and appreciate them.

If singing stardom is your goal . . . terrific. If you just want to be able to sing "Happy Birthday" at parties without embarrassing yourself . . . that's great too.

Let me introduce myself. My name is Roger Love, and I'm your new voice coach. Over the last twenty-five years I've had the pleasure of teaching some of the biggest superstars in the music and entertainment industry. When I was sixteen years old I was coaching the Beach Boys; the Jacksons; Earth, Wind & Fire; and the Fifth Dimension. Since then I've worked with rock groups like Def Leppard, Smashing Pumpkins, Papa Roach, Scorpions, Mötley Crüe, Poison, Cinderella, and Phish. And pop groups like Chicago, Toto, Wilson Phillips, Hanson, and Matchbox Twenty, along with teen stars like Mandy Moore, and R&B groups like En Vogue. Some of my most recent projects include the Ataris, Lisa Marie Presley, Xzibit, and Eminem. But there's a new student that I'm really excited about: *You.*

That's right, you're my next singing star, and I'm ready and able to turn your secret dreams of singing into reality. Maybe you want to sound better in the shower, or you think you've got what it takes to be the next *American Idol.* Either way, I promise it'll be

some of the most fun you ever had with your mouth open. Oh, and by the way, you're not tone deaf, so stop telling people that you are. Less than 2 percent of the population is actually tone deaf, so that excuse is not going to work anymore.

Inside your throat there's a beautiful instrument dying to get out. If you were born with a great natural voice—fantastic. But just so you know, most famous singers were not that lucky. Many successful recording artists were born with average talent. However, in order to succeed, they needed to work harder than everyone else, overcome the obstacles, never give up, deal with the hardships, and learn any secrets they could.

Secrets

"Secrets" are what this book is all about. Why would you want to spend years trying to learn something you can achieve in hours? The secrets I'll show you will change your voice so fast, you'll think that you've experienced a little bit of magic. All day long people come to my studio expecting a miracle, and I have to give them one. No, I can't part the Red Sea or change water to wine. I can, however, give you three octaves of range, in tune, with vibrato, diaphragmatic breathing, and no pressure. Which basically translates into your being able to sing just about any song you've ever heard, better than you'd ever imagined possible. The secrets I have for you will work. I've spent my professional life searching for and creating a system that makes it all possible.

Sound too good to be true? Let the facts sing for themselves. Over the last ten years I've vocal coached artists with more than a hundred million in album sales. That's something no other voice coach in the world has ever done, and I'm very proud of that. Having your own voice coach is a good thing. Just ask Eminem.

One More Chance

No matter what your history is, or how many times you've tried and failed to sing, I challenge you to take one more chance. This time we're going to make it through to the other side. I see a microphone and an audience in your future, and the crowd is standing on their feet smiling and screaming your name, and the good news is . . . they don't want their money back.

I remember about four years ago when I got a call from the head of A&R for Mercury Records. He told me about a family singing group from Oklahoma that he was working with and excited about. The lead singer had recorded half a song six months earlier in an extremely high key, but now his voice had changed. The record company loved the way the first part of the song sounded and didn't want to rerecord the song in a lower key. But no matter what they tried, there was no way he could hit the high notes. He went to sleep one night sounding like Minnie Mouse, and woke up the next morning sounding like Barry White. They'd been to just about every voice coach from Oklahoma to New York City, and no one could fix the problem. Before he gave up on the song altogether, he decided to take one more chance. He asked me to come to the studio that night and see if I could turn back the hands of time.

Within the next three hours we had successfully managed to finish the song. That night I got a lot of credit and a contract to vocal produce the rest of the album. The lead singer's name was Taylor, the group was Hanson, and the song was "MMMBop." It ended up being their debut single, launching their career, selling millions of records, and being nominated for a Grammy as the Best Song of the Year.

Not interested in selling records or winning Grammy awards? That's OK. All you want to do is sing karaoke with your friends? Fine.

My goal is to make you the best you can be, and to make it easy for you to achieve that goal. Whatever you do with your new talent is between you and your voice. I'm simply here to make sure that you have the time of your life,

I was asked by Eminem's agent and his personal manager to fly out to New York, meet with Eminem, and get his voice ready for the tour he was about to start—"The Eminem Show." So I left Los Angeles the very next day, flew into JFK International Airport, drove over five hours in rush-hour traffic, finally got to the venue—and his tour manager told me that Eminem had changed his mind. He decided that he didn't want to work with a vocal coach. "You've got to be kidding," I said. "I've been traveling for over twelve hours, and you've already prepaid me thousands of dollars for the next few days." He thought about the money thing for a second, and then decided that I was right, and he would see about hooking us up. He ushered me into a small dressing room behind the stage at the arena, and asked me to hang out for a few minutes while he set it up with Marshall. I put my suitcase on the ground, found a safe place to park my

electronic keyboard, and sat down to catch my breath. A few minutes later the tour manager came back to tell me that Eminem had agreed to meet with me. He then went on to add that I couldn't bring my keyboard in, that Marshall would never do any of that "lesson" stuff. And as if there weren't already enough rules, he told me that Marshall would never look me in the eyes when we were speaking, that he just doesn't do that. At that point I was hungry, tired, frustrated, and wondering why I'd left my incredibly cushy life at home for this craziness. But I put a smile on my face, slipped my keyboard under my arm, just in case, and headed toward Eminem's dressing room to meet him. The tour manager said he would check up on us after about five minutes to see if Marshall wanted me to leave, and I was wondering to myself, Could this get any worse? Then I walked in, met him, and do you know what happened next? Surprisingly, we really hit it off.

After five minutes he was doing all of the vocal exercises with the piano and me. We worked on diaphragmatic breathing, and one by one, I went through his songs, imitating him, and then showing him other ways to sing with less pressure and strain. The goal was to make sure that he could rap or sing every night and never lose his voice. He was amazed at what I could do with my voice, and he was more than willing to learn how to do it himself. It was *fantastic,* and he was very, very nice to me, not to mention the fact that after about fifteen minutes he even started

and more fun than you could have ever imagined. Believe me, when it comes to singing, it's definitely worth one more chance.

To Be or Not to Be

You'd probably be amazed at how many celebrities actually dream of becoming singers. Actors like Bruce Willis, Antonio Banderas, Sylvester Stallone, Kevin Spacey, Dennis Quaid, Keanu Reeves, Kelsey Grammer, Matthew Broderick, Gwyneth Paltrow, Catherine Zeta-Jones, Sarah Jessica Parker, Cybill Shepard, Renée Zellwegger, Jennifer Love Hewitt, Winona Ryder, Hilary Duff (from *The Lizzie McGuire Movie),* John and Rebecca Romijn-Stamos—and the list goes on and on, including one very famous supermodel who came to study with me, Tyra Banks.

Celebrity Tidbits

While I was writing this book, I decided to reach out to several of the most famous singers in the world, asking them to contribute some of their personal thoughts, tips, and advice. So throughout the book you'll see "Celebrity Tidbit" sections that do exactly that. This gives us a rare opportunity to hear directly from the stars themselves. They offer us advice on everything from proper breathing, to diet, to establishing your own original style. Each "Tidbit" also has a

"What do I think about that" section, where we talk a little more about what the celebrity said. Let me give you an example of how it works:

Celebrity Tidbit

I asked superstar **Luther Vandross** what was the funniest or most interesting thing that ever happened to him while he was singing, and here's what he said:

I'm a workaholic. Once, a new engineer didn't have the proper stamina and fell asleep at the control board.

I think that most people have no idea how hard it is to travel from city to city and stage a gigantic arena show every night. It's hard to sleep on a moving bus. It's a miracle that more people working as the crew don't fall asleep in the middle of every show.

✶ ✶ ✶ ✶ ✶ ✶ ✶ ✶ ✶

How to Use This Book and the CD

First of all, realize that I've given you everything you need to really learn how to sing. This is not just a book, it's an audio program as well. Read from chapter to chapter and follow along with

looking straight into my eyes when we spoke to one another. The manager kept coming in every ten minutes just to see if both of us were alive. He couldn't believe that Marshall was actually working like that with me. He had never imagined him being so willing and so open to this kind of voice coaching. The five minutes I was promised turned into almost an hour. He went on to sing that night using all of my pointers and felt great. The next day his voice wasn't strained at all. And that was the beginning of my Eminem story.

On the days that Tyra would come to my studio and take a lesson, people in my building lined the halls. Now, I've had plenty of gorgeous women come to me over the years . . . Miss Americas, Miss Californias, Miss Universes, some of the most beautiful women in the world. Still, everybody really wanted to catch a glimpse of Ms. Banks.

She was happy with her modeling career, doing a lot of acting, working hard on her charity work, and yet there was one true passion, one thing that she craved more than anything else—she wanted to be a singer. Deep down inside, the desire to be a singer was uncontrollable. She was working with a number of top producers and songwriters and putting together a demo tape to shop to record companies. She wanted to be the best she could be, so she decided to come and study with me.

When she sang for me, I knew there was something there to work with. As far as instruments go, she was born with a pretty good one. Her exercises were strong, on pitch, and she was able to move up and down the range without too many problems. She still needed me to strengthen her middle voice (the incredible, secret, life-changing, amazing voice I'll be teaching you in Chapter 3), so I did. She actually did the exercises a lot better than she sang songs, which is pretty common. So over the course of the next year we spent a lot of time together making sure that when she sang songs, she showcased her talents to the best of her abilities, and sounded great.

Tyra Banks is just one more perfect example of someone who has it all, and still wants to do whatever it takes to SING.

whatever I ask you to do or think about. Whenever I want you to listen to me, you'll see the following logo:

When you see that, you'll be directed to listen to a specific track on the enclosed CD. You have the written information, plus you have everything you need to hear on the CD. It's that simple.

You may want to find a nice comfortable place to read and to practice your vocal exercises, where you can make all kinds of sounds without bothering the rest of your family or your neighbors. But don't worry too much about your neighbors. In a week or so you'll be sounding so good, they'll have their ears pressed up against your window wondering who the new superstar singer is.

More . . . More . . . More

With *Sing Like The Stars* you *can* have the voice of your dreams, and sound just like the artists you love. The goal is to sing like a dream, breathe like a yoga instructor, lose your stage fright, find your original style, and look like a million bucks on stage . . . even if the stage is only in your living room.

There's even a chapter that'll teach you how to sing three megahit songs, using an incredible program I created called "Love Notes." I'll personally guide you through the process of learning and singing each of the songs. I'll coach you through the tough parts, and help you figure out exactly what to do with your new incredible voice.

When you put all this together you will have the most complete, effective, and entertaining singing system on the planet. I promise you it'll be a great experience. You may indeed be the next *American Idol*—and you didn't realize it was only one book away.

✳ ✳ ✳ ✳ ✳ ✳ ✳ ✳ ✳ ✳ ✳ ✳ ✳ ✳ ✳ ✳ ✳ ✳ ✳ ✳

Celebrity Tidbit

I asked superstar **Christina Aguilera** if there was one piece of advice she would offer to someone who wants to be a singer, and here's what she said:

It's always worked for me to just sing from the heart.

Great singers love to sing; it makes them happy. So even though I'm teaching you the greatest techniques in the world, in the end, like Christina says, you still need to sing from your heart.

✳ ✳ ✳ ✳ ✳ ✳ ✳ ✳ ✳ ✳ ✳ ✳ ✳ ✳ ✳ ✳ ✳ ✳ ✳ ✳

A Note of Caution

Just remember *never* to create any pressure or strain when you sing. As you sing along with the book and CD, make sure that you stop if it ever hurts. If you feel any pain at all, you're doing it wrong. If you have any discomfort, STOP, listen to my demonstrations on the CD, and then try it again. If it still feels bad, move on and come back to that specific thing later. In the end, everything will come together . . . I promise.

BREATHING

chapter TWO

papa ROACH

I was sitting in my office happily searching the Internet for nothing in particular when the manager of a group called Papa Roach called me. Interesting name, I thought.

Anyway, he wanted me to work with the lead singer Coby Dick. He was having some vocal problems live and in the studio. He sent me over a CD to listen to, and when I did, I realized what the problem was. Coby was screaming at the top of his lungs, forcing his voice to sound edgy and dark, and last but not least, he was holding his breath while he was singing.

When he came in to my studio I decided to fix the breathing problem first. His music was so aggressive that it forced him to blast out loud, angry sounds that created a lot of pressure and strain. Whenever he got louder, he also tightened his stomach muscles and held his breath. I told him that he needed to be more like a balloon.

When you blow air into a balloon it gets bigger, and if you hold the top closed, the air stays in there. When you let the top open up, the air comes out and the balloon gets small again. Pretty simple stuff, right? Well, breathing for singing is that simple too. When you take a breath in you're supposed to fill up your stomach as if you have a bal-

loon in there. Then when you sing out, your stomach is supposed to fall back in to its normal position.

I showed Coby how to do that and it made a world of difference. Now when he went for a higher note, instead of tightening his stomach, he would let it come in a little at a time. That really helped to take away a lot of the pressure. With the pressure gone, it was a lot easier to sing. He ended up being a terrific student, and over the next year we worked together quite often. The debut album went on to sell millions of copies. As long as he practiced the daily warm-up tape I made for him, he never had any vocal problems again. But remember, it all started with breathing, and not just any breathing . . .

Diaphragmatic Breathing

Diaphragmatic breathing sounds so scary, and besides that . . . it's hard to spell. But I can show you how simple it is to make breathing your new best friend. Think about it: Without the right amount of air coming out of your mouth, you can't sing at all.

You probably don't realize it, but sometimes when you try to sing, especially when you go to hit a high note, you're tightening your stomach and holding your breath just like Coby from Papa Roach, and that's making it a lot harder on you.

Great breathing leads to great singing, and I'd like to show you the secrets. The first of which is . . .

Always Breathe in Through Your Nose

Open your mouth and take a big deep breath in. Do you feel how the back part of your throat felt really dry when the air came through? That's not good.

Now close your mouth and take a big deep breath in through your nose. Do you feel how that *doesn't* make the back part of your throat feel dry? That's good.

Inside your nose there are little filters called turbinates. When the air passes through those filters it becomes moistened. Then when it gets to the vocal cords, the air doesn't dry them out as much. That's why breathing in through the nose is the only way to go.

Keeping your vocal cords happy is all about keeping them moist and lubricated. After all, how far can a car go when it's completely out of motor oil?

When you breathe in through your mouth it dries out all of the moisture sitting on the vocal cords. So when you sing, the cords easily get red and swollen, which makes you sound bad, and makes it a lot easier for you to lose your voice.

Many students say to me that they can't get enough air in through the nose. They feel that because one nostril is usually stuffed up, they can only get a small amount of air in.

Do you feel like that?

If so, I still want you to breathe in through your nose. Remember, you're only taking one breath at a time. I'm not asking you to take one big breath that'll last for ten minutes. All you have to do is to sing a few words of a song, and get ready to take the next breath. So whatever air you bring in through your nose will be more than enough to get you through the next set of words you need to sing. Besides, there's always some air in the lungs, so you never really have to fill up the tank all the way from empty.

Water and the Waiter

Great breathing is not about trying to fill your entire body full of air with each breath. It's more like a glass of water and a professional waiter. Let me explain. Whenever I have dinner at a great restaurant I notice that my water glass always has water in it. During the course of the evening, even though I'm drinking from the glass, the waiter still manages to come by often and fill it so that I never run out. He wants a big tip, and I'm more likely to give him one if the service is good. He never waits for me to finish all the water and then fill the glass from empty. Great breathing is just like that. You take air in, use some of it to sing a few words, and then take another breath, filling up whatever space is left to fill inside the lungs. I want you to get used to taking as many breaths as possible. Being a good singer is

all about sending a solid stream of air out of the mouth. Taking a lot of breaths really helps to accomplish that.

Good and Bad Breathing

There are two different ways to breathe. One is good for you, and the other is a big waste of time.

I want you to go somewhere in your house where you have a big mirror. Then, on the count of 3, take a deep breath and watch your upper body in the mirror: 1—2—3.

Did you raise your chest and shoulders? If so, that's called *accessory breathing,* and that's the way to get the least amount of air in and out.

Now put your hand on your stomach where your belly button is, and this time when you breathe in, pretend that you have a balloon in your stomach. As you inhale, let your stomach come out and fill the balloon with air.

Try it again, but this time, make sure that you don't raise your chest and shoulders. One more time:

1. Put your hand on your belly button.
2. Take a big breath in and pretend that you have a balloon in your stomach.
3. Fill up that balloon with air.
4. Exhale and let your stomach fall back in to its normal position.

This is called *diaphragmatic breathing,* and it's perfect for your body and your singing.

When you're driving a car, and you want that car to go fast, what do you have to do? Push down on the accelerator pedal. The more you push the pedal down, the faster the car goes.

Diaphragmatic breathing goes something like that. When you want the air to come out fast, you just bring your stomach in fast. When you want the air to come out slowly, you just let your stomach come back in slowly. This way, you're in total control of how much air is coming out when you sing, and by the way . . . this is very important.

If you become good at controlling how the air flows out of your mouth, you're going to be able to sing a million times better than you do now. Your singing will ride out on a solid bed of air and sound incredible.

Practice diaphragmatic breathing until it becomes second nature. You already knew how to do it perfectly earlier in your life. All babies are born with expert breathing skills, even you. But somewhere along the way, you stopped breathing properly like a child, and started imitating adults who breathe the wrong way and it's definitely time we went back the right way.

* *

Celebrity Tidbit

luther VANDROSS

I asked superstar **Luther Vandross** if he had any breathing advice for us, and here's what he said:

The proper way to breathe is on your back, on the floor. It makes the abdomen work correctly.

I think Luther is right on the money. When you lay down on your back, especially when you raise your knees up a little bit, your body moves into a terrific position to get a lot of air into the lungs. Also, when you're lying on your back, it's easier to feel and watch your stomach fill like a balloon. That's great for diaphragmatic breathing.

* *

Posture Is Important

When you raise your chest up and move your shoulders back and down, you can sing much better. Why is that? Well, it's because of the position of your rib cage. When you raise your chest up, your ribs move out of the way and let more air go into the lungs.

When you round over your shoulders and pretend that you're an inch shorter, the rib cage gets in the way and blocks a lot of the air from getting in.

Have you ever spoken with someone who had a bruised or broken rib? If so, you would have noticed that they spoke with almost no volume or power. That's because they couldn't get a big-enough breath in. Without the ability to move the rib cage out of the way, the situation was hopeless.

Making sure that your chest is up, your shoulders back and down, and your feet

about shoulder-width apart will get you a lot closer to having good posture. Play around with it and you'll notice some positive changes.

It Makes Me Look Fat

Sometimes people say to me they won't do diaphragmatic breathing because it makes them look fat.

Are you worried about that?

If so, *don't be.* Remember that your audience is usually in front of you. When they're watching you from the front and you fill your stomach up with air, they don't even notice the movement. They're not on the side of you, staring at your stomach. Besides, if you look in the mirror and watch yourself when you breathe and raise your chest and shoulders way up, that looks a lot more distracting!

When Air Meets the Vocal Cords

Now I want to explain a bit more of why air and proper breathing are so important for singing.

Great singing only happens when the right amount of air meets the right amount of vocal cord. Let me show you what I mean by this:

1. **Make a peace sign with your fingers and face your hand toward you.**
2. **Bring your fingers really close to your lips.**
3. **Now blow air easily right through the open space between your two fingers. That's basically what happens when the vocal cords are open and the air blows right through. If you sang with the cords in this position you would sound airy and breathy, like Mariah Carey does when she sings down low.**
4. **Now close your fingers together and continue to try to blow air through. Do you feel how your fingers block the air? That's basically what the cords are doing in the closed position. If you sang with the cords like that, you would sound edgy, thick, and powerful, like Sting.**

5. Now close your fingers again and try to blow the air through, then after a second spread your two fingers back apart into the peace sign, and then close your fingers again.

Open—closed—open—closed—open—closed. That's really what's happening when you're singing. Air comes up to the closed cords and tries to push its way through. Eventually the cords give in, and a little burst of air comes through. As soon as the air comes through, the cords close back up again and the whole process starts over. These little airbursts that escape through the cords are what makes up sound. The amazing thing is, when you sing, the cords do that little open-close dance anywhere from 200 to 2,000 times a second.

When people come up to me and say that they're always worried that their voice might crack or break, I tell them how lucky they really are. They don't realize that 2,000 times a second something could go wrong but usually doesn't.

✳ ✳

Celebrity Tidbit

brian McKNIGHT

I asked superstar **Brian McKnight** if he had any breathing advice for us, and here's what he said:

I believe if you stay in good physical health your breathing should be normal and help you sing your best.

If you learn to breathe correctly when you exercise, especially if you're doing any type of cardiovascular workout, diaphragmatic breathing can really help you out. So Brian and I totally agree . . staying in good health and breathing correctly will always lead to better singing.

✳ ✳

You and the Accordion

Learning how to do diaphragmatic breathing is an important part of singing. Once you get good at it, you'll be in a position to really make the most out of your singing voice.

Remember, it's all about trying to get the air down low where your belly button is. And as you sing, you have to concentrate on your stomach coming back in to its normal position. You can't just take a big breath of air, fill up your stomach, and then keep it out while you sing.

Have you ever seen an accordion? It's that handheld keyboard next to the monkey with the little hat and vest. To play an accordion, you have to bring both hands apart. This makes air go into the instrument. Then as you bring your hands back in toward one another, music and air come out of the accordion. That outward and inward movement is what great breathing is all about. If you—or the accordion—stay in the out position, the show is over.

When you're singing and you go for a high note, you need to make extra sure that you don't stop your stomach from coming in like a good accordion. With your stomach coming in the whole time you're singing, every note in the song will be there for you at your command.

Breathing Exercises

Before we leave the breathing chapter I want to give you a couple of great exercises to practice with. Play around with them and your breathing will definitely improve.

I call the first one the SLOW LEAK:

1. Take a breath in through your nose and fill up your stomach like a balloon.
2. With your teeth together and lips slightly apart make an *sss* sound like the beginning of the word "snake."
3. With your hand on your stomach let the smallest amount of air possible out of your mouth while you continually make the *sss* sound. Try to hold it out for as long as you can.
4. Take another breath and try to hold it out even longer. Make sure that your stomach is slowly coming in without any tension.

Note: The goal here is not to pass out. We're simply getting used to a little bit of air coming out, and the stomach slowly falling back to its normal position.

I call the next exercise the BIRTHDAY CANDLE:

1. Take a breath in through your nose and fill up your stomach like a balloon.
2. Pretend that you are in front of a birthday cake with one candle on it.
3. Let your stomach come in a tiny bit and let one small burst of air come out of your mouth, as if you were blowing out a candle that was about a foot in front of you.
4. Right after you blow the small burst of air, close your mouth and get ready to blow out the next candle.
5. Continue to let small air bursts come out one at a time until you run out of air, then just take a new breath and start all over again.

Recap . . .

Remember . . . you should be doing diaphragmatic breathing all the time, not just when you're singing. If you've ever taken a yoga class I'm sure the instructor tried to get you to breathe the same way. This type of breathing is incredibly good for your body. Many people believe that diaphragmatic breathing actually helps to oxygenate the blood, something that's very good for your overall health.

So, if we can make your body and your singing stronger, Let's go for it!

THE MAGIC OF CHEST, MIDDLE, AND HEAD VOICE

chapter THREE

lisa marie PRESLEY

Some time ago I was hired to teach **Lisa Marie Presley** how to sing. There were rumors flying all around town about her signing with Capitol Records and getting ready to record her debut album. After all, how many Elvis Presleys were there, and how many daughters did he have? Even I was excited about hearing what she could do. The producer who originally set us up told me I was going to be pleasantly surprised, and he was right. I thought she had a very interesting voice, especially on the low end, and I was impressed by how much vocal style she already had. Her voice was unique, and she sang with a great deal of emotion and soul. Realizing that she was only strong in the lower part of her voice, however, I immediately started building all of the middle and higher notes. She was a terrific student and we had a great deal of success making sure that she could go from low to high perfectly, without any pressure. She went on to make her debut album, which was a big seller all across the country.

I'm going to teach you exactly what I taught her, and when we're done, maybe people will be calling you the new king or queen or rock 'n' roll, or maybe you'll just get the first piece of cake after you sing "Happy Birthday."

Magic Middle

Most people think there are only two voices: chest voice, down low where you speak, and head voice, way up high where you don't speak.

When you sing a song that goes from really low to really high, does your voice kind of freak out?

Do you break or crack, or sound funny in the middle?

Do you sound like one person on the bottom and then a totally different person on the top?

Well, that's *not* the way it's supposed to be.

What you probably don't know is there's another voice called *middle voice* that lives right in between the low and high parts of your voice. And if you don't have middle, there's no way to sing from low to high without pressure, strain, and a big goofy break. But with a middle voice you can suddenly sing all the way up and down the keyboard. Songs that were only a dream before will now be within reach.

**(PLEASE LISTEN TO MY DEMONSTRATION
ON TRACK 2 OF THE CD)**

When you listen to Christina Aguilera or Celine Dion sing up high, they're in middle voice.

When you listen to Luther Vandross or Sting sing up high, they're in middle voice. I can make that happen for you.

I can't stress enough how important the middle voice is. I've spent twenty-five years concentrating on it and helping people find it. It's the most important part of my technique, and the number one thing I want you to learn from me. When you own a middle voice, you'll be able to sing songs you never thought possible. It's the magic, the diamond, and the pot of gold at the end of the rainbow. All of the best singers in the world use middle voice, and you will too.

Before I teach you how to find the middle, I want to first find out which of the following two types of singers *you* are.

Are You Trapped in Chest Voice?

Some people think that *chest voice* is king. They start out singing down low, feeling bold, strong, and carefree like a train running downhill. But as the notes get higher, they start to feel pressure. They look all over their body for help. They tighten their stomach muscles and pray for support, they squeeze their buttocks together, their two eyebrows become one, and they feel about six feet tall in a room where the ceiling is only six feet high.

Suddenly the train is now having a much harder time getting up a new steep hill. So they get louder and louder and use whatever energy they can find to try to push out the higher notes. But even if some of the higher notes come out, they still sound strained, like they're shouting.

**(PLEASE LISTEN TO MY DEMONSTRATION
ON TRACK 3 OF THE CD)**

Is this how you feel when you try to sing strong and high? If so, you're going to love having a middle voice. I'll show you how to get out of the chest voice when you're supposed to, and move seamlessly into the middle, and then into the head voice.

Right now when you sing, it's a bit like being at the gym lifting weights. As the notes get higher, each one feels heavier and heavier. But great singing is not like weight lifting. It's not supposed to be harder to hit the higher notes. Once you have a middle voice, all that pressure and strain will be a distant memory.

Or Are You Head Voice Queen?

A lot of women who have studied with classical teachers think that *head voice* is really a feminine thing. The teachers have them believing that all great singers need a classical

background. They have them listen to opera divas who spend all of their time singing high in head voice and never sing down low where the rest of the population actually speaks. The problem is, when you try to bring your head voice down too low, it loses all of its strength.

(PLEASE LISTEN TO MY DEMONSTRATION ON TRACK 4 OF THE CD)

Now don't get me wrong here. I think studying classical singing and music is fantastic. It's just that I don't want you to get stuck in any one of the three main voices all of the time. I'm trying to teach you that to have the greatest voice, you need to own chest voice down low, middle voice in the middle, and head voice on the high notes.

Are you stuck in head voice? Do you sound pretty on the high notes and then as you come down the range get softer and softer until you fade into nothingness? If so, don't worry about it. The CD warm-up exercises will help you add the chest and middle to the head voice you already own.

Just remember that the warm-up exercises are your ticket to making gigantic positive changes in your voice. Anybody and everybody who's a great singer uses vocal exercises to make things better. Take a look at what **Cher** says about vocal warm-ups.

✳ ✳ ✳ ✳ ✳ ✳ ✳ ✳ ✳ ✳ ✳ ✳ ✳ ✳ ✳ ✳ ✳ ✳ ✳

Celebrity Tidbit

cher

I asked superstar **Cher** what she does to warm up her voice before a performance, and if she'd ever taken any singing lessons, and here's what she said:

I warm up with a tape from my vocal coach before I sing, and though I started studying late in my career, both my coaches have dramatically changed my vocal ability.

It's so nice when students give credit to their teachers. I've learned over the years that the right exercises and technique can make the difference between a good singer and an incredible one. Warm-up exercises are the fastest way to get you and your voice to where they need to be.

Finding Your Voices

Now let's do an exercise to help you find your chest, middle, and head voices. Just sing along with me and follow what I do. I call it the ONE-OCTAVE GOOG.

(ALL WOMEN, AND ANY MEN WHOSE VOICES HAVEN'T CHANGED YET, PLEASE LISTEN TO TRACK 5 ON THE CD)

(ALL MEN WHOSE VOICES HAVE CHANGED, PLEASE LISTEN TO TRACK 6 ON THE CD)

Note: Don't worry if the GOOG exercise was difficult or you got a bit confused. We're only at the beginning of our work together. I promise you'll still win the race.

Where Does Middle Voice Live on the Piano?

If you look at the following illustrations, you'll see exactly where chest, middle, and head voice are on the piano. Most people are a bit surprised when they see that the middle voice is really only a small area compared with chest and head. For a man, the chest voice usually starts at around low E or F, which is twelve or thirteen white keys below middle C. It goes up for about two octaves (twenty-three or twenty-four notes), reaching middle voice at around the E or F above middle C. Middle voice runs from that E or F to about B-flat or B-natural. Above that, from C and beyond, you're in head voice.

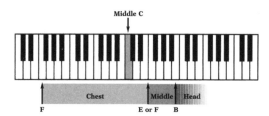

For women: Chest voice starts at the F below middle C and continues up for about seventeen notes to the B-flat above middle C. Middle voice covers the next six notes or so, and then ends at around E or F; higher than that is head voice.

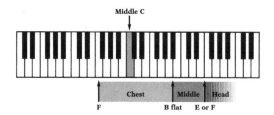

Everybody Needs a Middle Voice . . . Even Rob Thomas

No matter what type of songs you love to sing, you still need a middle voice. Even if you spend all of your time down low where you speak, you still need one. I want to make it so that you can sing anywhere up and down the range feeling as free as a bird. I want you to feel like you're six feet tall and the ceiling is twenty-five feet high. That way you'll never bump your head.

Let me tell you a story about one of my students who was only using chest voice until I gave him middle. His name is Rob Thomas.

What Are Your Cords Doing?

I wanted to give you an idea of what the vocal cords are actually doing in chest, middle, and head voice. Not because I want you to be doctors; it's just that I believe that when you know what's going on, it's easier to accomplish something. If you're in the dark, it's hard to find the instructions written on the walls. So here goes . . .

I want you to think of a grand piano. Can you picture the shape in your mind? Do you see how one side of the piano is really long, and the other side is much shorter? That's because the longer side of the piano has much longer strings. And not only are they longer, they're also a lot thicker. The long thick strings on the piano make the low bassy sounds. The shorter and thinner the strings get, the higher the notes.

Do you follow me here?

If you sat down at a piano and pushed down the farthest key on the right side, it would make a cute, high little "ping" kind of noise. That's the shortest string. Vice versa, if you hit the key all the way at the farthest left side of the piano keyboard, it would sound more like a low "boom." So with regard to sound, size does matter. The size and thickness of the string are directly proportionate to how low or high the note is.

I was sitting in my office waiting for the next student to come when the phone rang. It was the manager of George Michael, Terence Trent D'Arby, and Matchbox Twenty. Today he was calling me because one of his clients, Rob Thomas, the lead singer of Matchbox Twenty, was having vocal problems. They had just finished recording the album *Yourself or Someone Like You* and they were playing live shows around town. Rob's voice was perfect for the first two shows of the week, but after that he got hoarse, sounded like he was losing his voice, and had to shout out all of the higher notes. His manager asked me if I could make it so that he could perform five and six nights a week and always sound great. I told him I would give it a shot.

When Rob came to my studio and I did a couple of vocal exercises with him, I realized that he had an incredibly strong chest voice but no middle at all. He had charisma, style, and starlike presence. He was a great musician, and could easily write hit songs one after another. But he still needed a middle voice. Whenever he was singing and had to hit a high note, he would just try to push his chest voice up too high. That was putting way too much pressure on his cords and making them red and swollen. After a couple of days of that, his voice was in no shape at all to give the audience what they came for.

I gave him some vocal exercises to find his middle voice, and then showed him how to use that middle voice in his songs. I also made a special tape for him to practice every morning. Following that tape, he could make sure that he always had chest, middle, and head voice perfectly connected. Within a week he was performing every night, sounding great, and not losing his voice.

By the way, I have the perfect warm-up tape for you, too. The CD that comes along with this book has a daily warm-up section that'll help you make your voice better every day you practice. Just sing along with the CD and follow my instructions. You'll have a lot of fun, and in no time at all, you'll find your middle voice.

A few weeks later I went to a Matchbox Twenty performance in Los Angeles and their

You should think of the vocal cords as if they were like parts of a zipper. When you're in chest voice, the vocal cords are vibrating their full length, like the long strings of a piano. When you start to go higher, there's a process called *dampening* that closes off part of the cords, just like a zipper partially closing. When the zipper is about halfway closed, you're in middle voice. As the zipper closes about three-quarters of the way, you're in head voice.

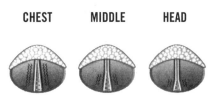

CHEST   MIDDLE   HEAD

Even though the actual process of the vocal cords moving from chest to middle to head voice is much more complicated, I feel like the zipper analogy is an easy way for you to visualize it all.

Then What the Heck Is Falsetto?

I just explained that the vocal cords vibrate long in chest, shorter in middle, and even shorter in head voice. So, where does falsetto fit into all of this? Did you think that falsetto was just another word for head voice? Well, it's not. *Falsetto* happens when the vocal cords move mostly out of the way and let a gigantic amount of air come thundering through. Then, instead of the normal part of the cords working, only the outer edge vibrates. Some artists actually use the falsetto sound as a big part of their style. Groups like the Beach Boys, the Bee Gees, and Earth, Wind & Fire all used a ton of falsetto in their original sounds.

In the beginning when you work on the CD warm-up exercises that come along with this book, don't worry about falsetto. In fact, stay away from it, at least for a while, until I can make your chest, middle, and head voices perfect. If I let you start to go to falsetto now, you'll never end up with a strong middle. You'll be bouncing back and forth between weak and strong sounds, and you'll only get confused. Later, after your middle is unbelievable, you can sing all the falsetto you want.

(PLEASE LISTEN TO MY DEMONSTRATION OF FALSETTO ON TRACK 7 OF THE CD)

Vocal Autopilot

So, your job as you sing from low to high is to let the vocal cords vibrate long and thick in chest voice and then let them get shorter for middle,

manager came up to me and thanked me for saving his artist's life. I told him, "I didn't save his life, I just gave him a middle voice." "Same thing," he said, and then introduced me to the Atlantic Records A&R executive who signed the band, saying, "This is Roger Love, the guy who just made sure that your kids are going to be able to continue going to private school."

Matchbox Twenty went on over the next few years to sell more than 60 million albums. Rob never had another vocal problem again.

and even shorter for head voice. Sounds complicated, doesn't it? Well, the good news is that your voice is actually set up to do all of that by itself. It's ready at any time to go into autopilot without your having to worry about a thing. That is, if you follow some very simple rules:

1. **Stop getting louder as you get higher. In the chapter on breathing, we learned that the vocal cords love it when you send a solid, even stream of air toward them. Whenever a big, sudden burst of air comes up to the vocal cords, they respond by bracing themselves and trying desperately to stop the air from getting through. When you get louder as you go higher, you increase the amount of air coming to the cords. When that happens, they lock in the chest voice position and can't move to the shorter middle voice place. That gets you and your voice stuck in chest with a ton of pressure and strain.**

(PLEASE LISTEN TO MY DEMONSTRATION ON TRACK 8 OF THE CD)

   It's so much better if you just keep the same volume when you're trying to sing the higher notes. That way the cords don't lock, and the "zipper" is free to move without getting stuck in one position.

2. **Stop locking the top part of your stomach. When you're trying to sing from chest voice (down low) to middle voice (up higher), you need to make sure that nothing happens to block the even flow of air. When you tighten the muscles at the top part of your stomach you create a tourniquet effect, like a hose with a big knot in it, and the air has a hard time getting through. When that happens you get stuck in chest voice with no way to get to middle. You need to make sure that your stomach is always coming in as you sing out. The second that the top part of the stomach tightens and remains still, your chances of middle voice are dead and buried.**

3. Make sure that your larynx doesn't go up. Before you can stop it from going up, you probably need to know what it is and where it is. The *larynx* is the voice box, and if you put your index finger on your chin and slide it backward until you hit a little bump, that would be it. Well, technically the bump is your Adam's apple, which is the front part of your larynx. Still, the larynx has two jobs. First, it's the house for the vocal cords; they live in there and are protected by it. And second, the larynx is part of the swallowing function. There are two holes in the back part of your throat, one for food and liquid and the other for air. When you swallow, the larynx comes up and closes off the air hole so that food or liquid doesn't go down there and choke you. Put your finger on your Adam's apple again and swallow. Do you feel it jump up above your finger and then come back down? When your larynx comes up like that, the throat closes and it becomes impossible to find the middle voice. You'll either end up stuck in chest voice, or you have a big break as you go from chest to head and miss the middle voice altogether.

(PLEASE LISTEN TO MY DEMONSTRATION OF THE LOW-LARYNX SOUND ON TRACK 9 OF THE CD)

By following these three rules . . .

✶ Not getting louder as you get higher.
✶ Not locking the top part of your stomach.
✶ Not letting your larynx jump up.

. . . You have a much greater chance of connecting your chest voice to your middle to your head voice. With that done, you can sing just about any song, no matter where the notes of the song go.

Celebrity Tidbit

I asked superstar **Brian McKnight** if he thought aspiring singers should take singing lessons, and here's what he said:

I think if you don't know how to sing the proper way, you need a vocal coach.

I believe that everything is much easier when you have the right information. That's what a good coach and technique can offer.

Now, let's do another exercise to strengthen your chest, middle, and head voices. I call it the ONE-OCTAVE GUG.

(ALL FEMALES, AND ANY MALES WHOSE VOICES HAVEN'T CHANGED YET, PLEASE GO TO TRACK 10 ON THE CD)

(ALL MALES WHOSE VOICES HAVE CHANGED, PLEASE GO TO TRACK 11 ON THE CD)

Just like before, follow along with me and do what I do. After you try it once, come back and read the following tips and then go back to the CD and try it again.

If It Hurts, You're Doing It Wrong. So How Are You Doing?

You're not supposed to feel any pain or pressure as you go from chest to middle to head. How did it feel when you did the GUG exercise above?

Did you . . . get to the top of your chest voice and then freak out?

If so, you need to make sure that you're at least trying to leave chest voice and look for middle. You need to concentrate on getting out of chest voice and going anywhere you can, even if it breaks into an airy, light head voice. The goal is to leave chest voice before you start feeling any pain or pressure.

Think of it like this. There you are in your living room thinking about going into the bedroom. You get up off the sofa, walk down the hall and into the bedroom—no sweat. Chest voice is like the living room, head voice is the bedroom, and middle voice is the hall. It's as easy as can be to go from the living room through the hall to the bedroom. But, try going from the living room to the bedroom without going down the hall. It's a lot harder, if not impossible. When you're singing in chest voice and going higher, you need to look for middle and leave the chest behind, the same way you leave the living room and decide to go into the hall. It's a different room and a different voice.

Did you get louder as you went higher?

If so, you really need to focus on keeping the same volume. I know it's hard to do, but if you practice you can make it happen. Think of it like this. Imagine that you're sitting at a grand piano. When you move your right hand all the way over to the right side and press down a key, you hear a high note. You wouldn't feel any physical pain or tension to do that. Now imagine your left hand moving all the way to the left and pressing down a low-note key. That wouldn't physically hurt you either. Now imagine that same piano on its side lying on the ground with you lying right beside it. When you went to press down a low key you could easily reach it. But now, if you tried to hit a high key, you would have to stretch your arm all the way up, and that would be a lot harder. If you're sitting at a piano it's totally easy to play low and high notes. You just simply move your left or right hand into position. You need to think of singing in the same way. The high notes are *not* harder; you'll get used to moving the vocal cords as easily as you move your hands on the piano. Keeping the same volume as you sing from low to high will really help to make that a reality.

Did you try to push your chest voice up too high?

Remember, chest voice is just one of the three voices. No matter how much you love it,

it won't take you everywhere you want to go. Even though your middle and head voice might both be puny, you still need to give them some love and attention. Don't freak out when you try to leave chest and feel totally weak on the high notes. The warm-up exercises will take the weak sounds and turn them into something special—if you practice. Every day you leave chest voice and try to find the middle, your voice will get stronger and healthier.

Did you have a big break when your voice tried to go from chest to middle?

If so, understand that everybody has a break in the beginning. You're not just born with the ability to sing from low to high perfectly. You were given an instrument, but you still need to learn how to play it correctly.

Did you even find the middle voice?

You hear me saying, "Middle . . . middle . . . middle," and you try the exercises, but you still have no clue about this mysterious middle voice. You go to head voice and you think, This might be middle, then you bring chest voice up high and it hurts a little less so you think, This might be middle. Just remember, whenever you get confused, you should always go back to the CD and listen to my demonstrations. Imitating is the way to succeed. Listen to me over and over, and then just try to copy what you hear.

Also, you need to understand that middle voice is supposed to sound more like the chest voice. It's supposed to be big and strong and bassy and brassy, just like your speaking voice does. You know you've found the middle when you're singing high but you still sound like you're down low.

**(PLEASE LISTEN TO MY DEMONSTRATION
ON TRACK 12 OF THE CD)**

Did you let your larynx come up too high?

The middle voice can only shine if it becomes big and strong. The only way to make it strong is to keep the back part of your throat open. The only way to keep it open is to make sure that your larynx stays down. As soon as your larynx rises, your chances of finding the middle voice are slim to none. So do whatever it takes to keep your larynx down.

Add the Yogi Bear sound, or put your finger on your Adam's apple and try to keep it from rising too far when you sing.

Something Else to Chew On: Dropping Your Jaw

I don't know if you've noticed, but most people sing like they have lockjaw. They go to hit a high note and create a ton of pressure under the chin and around the jaw. But learning when and how to drop your jaw will help you go smoothly from chest to middle to head voice and eliminate some of the pressure.

Put your thumb on your chin and slide it backward for about an inch, and push upward. Count to ten with your finger right there pushed in under your chin: 1, 2, 3, 4, 5, 6, 7, 8, 9, 10.

Try it again and this time concentrate on what the muscles under your chin are doing. Are they moving? Are they pushing down with a lot of pressure? Probably not.

Now with your finger in the same position, sing "Ah" from very low to very high. Pay attention to the muscles and you'll probably feel them push downward as you sing toward the top part of your chest voice. When there's tension there, it's a lot harder to sing. So, what should you do to get rid of the pressure?

Drop your jaw.

Sounds too easy? Well . . . it is.

When you're going for a high note, you just need to drop your jaw down. Three things happen when you do that:

1. Dropping your jaw actually relieves the tension in the muscles right under your chin.
2. When you drop your jaw, you open up the very back part of your throat. That allows a solid, free amount of air to come through.

3. Dropping the jaw makes the sound bounce into your cheeks creating a bigger, fatter, fuller sound. Imagine a big bass drum. The sides are huge, and when you hit the top with your drumstick, the sound bounces all around the big space inside of the drum. That's what happens to the inside of your mouth when you drop your jaw . . . and that's a good thing.

SECRETS OF VIBRATO

chapter FOUR

def LEPPARD

I got a call from a manager in New York whose company represents Metallica, Def Leppard, and Courtney Love. He asked me if I wanted to fly to the island of Ibiza off the coast of Spain, stay there for a month or so, and work with his act Def Leppard. A week later I was unpacking my suitcase overlooking the most beautiful coastline I had ever seen. Def Leppard, in case you don't know, was one of the biggest-selling rock bands of all time. They had two albums in a row sell over 12 million copies each. In the eighties and early nineties they were huge all around the world.

My first day on the island I was supposed to meet Joe Elliott in the bar of the hotel at lunchtime, which was right about when he got up. By the way, the rumor that rock stars sleep in until noon is not a rumor. Anyway, we met and I instantly liked him very much. I told him about myself and the techniques I'd be teaching him. One of the things I mentioned was the word "vibrato." "I won't be needin' any of that," he said in a very thick English accent. "Why not?" I asked. "Because we don't use any of it," he replied. "What about when you hold out one note for a long time?" I asked, "We don't do that," he answered. At that moment I thought he was crazy. Later, however, I came to realize he was absolutely right. Most of the time when a singer holds out a note for a

long time, he usually adds vibrato—the wave-like movement that makes it sound more beautiful. But Def Leppard was not like everyone else. Instead of holding out a note, they would sing a note and then slide off it. I hadn't noticed it before, but now I realized it was indeed part of their signature style. They were the one group in a thousand who had created a unique sound without using any vibrato. Well, that's just peachy for Def Leppard, but it's not fine for *you*. I'll tell you exactly what I told him: "I'm going to teach it to you anyway, because it'll make you a much better singer. After you own it, you can use it or not, it's up to you." And just so you know, after I taught him how to do it, he used it plenty.

What It Is

When a great singer holds out a long note he or she sometimes has a little "wiggle" in their voice that adds richness and warmth. That wiggle is called *vibrato*. When you do it wrong, you sound like a sheep lost in the woods. When you do it right, you sound incredible.

Before I teach you how to do it, I want to explain further what it is and why you need it.

Vibrato is a wavelike oscillation of the pitch. Which means that as you hold out a note, the pitch moves up and down, higher and lower, like the waves of the ocean. When vibrato's right, the wave moves up and down about six times per second.

VIBRATO

One Second

This is really important to understand. **The speed of the vibrato makes all the difference in the world:** A little too fast—bad! A little too slow—bad! Six beats a second—you'll feel like the vibrato was a gift from God that just effortlessly happens whenever you open your mouth.

When you listen to a singer like Stevie Nicks or Madonna, you'll hear a vibrato that's a bit too fast. The fast vibrato makes the singer sound nervous and overly excited.

Fast vibrato doesn't add warmth and beauty to the voice. It simply makes the singer sound nervous and agitated.

On the other side of the fence, when the vibrato is too slow, it makes the singer sound like an old retired opera singer who can barely walk or talk. Listen to Liza Minnelli and you'll hear the slowest vibrato in town. She sounds like she's recording all of her vocals in a car riding down a street with speed bumps evenly spaced every fifteen feet.

(PLEASE LISTEN TO TRACK 13 ON THE CD AND HEAR ME DEMONSTRATE THE CORRECT VIBRATO, ALONG WITH THE TOO-SLOW AND TOO-FAST VERSIONS)

Why You Need It

Let's say you've decided to sing the song "My Heart Will Go On" from the movie *Titanic*, performed by Celine Dion. When you sing the words "We'll stay forever this way" and you stretch out the "Weeeee'll" and the "Staaaaaay," you can either stretch out the words and sing them straight, or you can add vibrato to the "We'll" and "Stay."

(PLEASE LISTEN TO MY DEMONSTRATION ON TRACK 14 OF THE CD)

Whenever you try to hold out (sustain) a long note without vibrato, you're going to realize that it's very difficult not to go flat. *Flat* is when you try to sing a particular note and it ends up going a little bit lower uncontrollably, which basically makes you sound like a car wreck. The reason it goes flat is because of the way that sound actually travels through the air.

Have you ever head the phrase *sound wave?* Why do you think it's called that?

It's literally because the sound moves through the air just like a wave pattern. It goes up and down in a regular, wavelike motion.

Do you see the similarity here? Sound travels in waves and vibrato is also a wave-like motion.

So, the reason it's hard to sing a long pitch without vibrato is because it's like trying to stop the natural wavelike movement of the sound. Are you with me?

Singing short notes is like sending out a straight little line of sound. But as soon as you sing the note longer, it wants to become a wave. When you don't let that happen, you're fighting against the laws of nature, and it just doesn't sound as good.

There's another really good reason to own a vibrato. As I said before, vibrato makes the note go up and down a bit. So if you are singing the note D, and you add vibrato, you would actually be singing a sound wave that would go up a little higher than the D, almost to the very next key on the piano, which in this case would be the D-sharp. Then the sound would go a bit lower than the D to the D-flat.

**(PLEASE LISTEN TO MY DEMONSTRATION
ON TRACK 15 OF THE CD)**

This movement of the pitch is a good thing, because it actually makes it easier for you to sing on pitch altogether.

Why is that?

For the same reason that you need a good nozzle on your hose when you're trying to wash the car. Let's say that you have a hose that only sends out a really tiny stream of water. No matter how hard and fast that water comes out, you can only get a little bit of the car wet at a time. Wherever you point the hose gets wet, but just one foot over is as dry as a bone. Singing *without* vibrato is kind of like that. You have to be perfectly in tune and on the specific pitch at every moment.

Now, imagine if the nozzle on your hose let you change the stream to a bigger, wider, rounder flow of water. You would be able to get more of the car wet at the same time. Singing *with* vibrato is kind of like that.

The vibrato makes the sound wave bigger and wider, like the hose nozzle did with the water. Therefore, when you go to hit a certain note, you have a much better chance of hitting it with that bigger wave of sound.

Anyway, that's more than enough technical info. The bottom line is, *vibrato is fun to make,* and it'll make you sound like a great singer. If you love to sing, you'll love singing with vibrato. Before I give you some exercises to help you find it, I want to give you a bit more information.

Vibrato's Bigger Than Musical Theater or Opera

Sometimes pop music students are afraid to add vibrato when they sing songs. They tell me that they don't want to sound like an opera singer or a musical theater performer. Somewhere along the way, they've connected the vibrato thing with a more classical-type voice and style. And even though opera and musical theater singers *do* usually have a lot of vibrato, that doesn't mean it's wrong for pop, or rock, or gospel, or R&B, or country music. Vibrato—used in the right way, in the right places, at the right speed—is a necessary part of every style of music, especially if you want to sound like you can sing.

Whatever It Takes

I want you to understand something: Some of the things I'm going to suggest are just temporary tricks or triggers to make the vibrato happen. If I let your stomach move in and out, it's only temporary. If I have you shake your hand, or jump up and down like a kernel in a popcorn machine, it's just to find the vibrato. Within reason, I'll do whatever it takes to give you the most incredible vibrato on the planet. But once we find it and you get used to it, I promise you won't be doing anything silly or awkward to keep it up.

Lots of singers, however, still do some pretty crazy things to make vibrato. For example, have you ever seen Whitney Houston singing live or on TV? Sometimes when she makes vibrato, she shakes her jaw like a piranha eating a hamburger. It moves up and down fast, and it looks very uncomfortable and unnatural.

So why does she do that?

The answer is, when she grew up, there were obviously a number of singers in her church choir that shook their jaw like that. Whitney, who is an amazing talent, is also incredible at imitating. In doing so, however, she picked up a few bad habits to go along with all of the good things she does. By the way, Whitney can also make vibrato perfectly without any of the jaw shaking. She only does it wrong some of the time.

When you shake your jaw to make vibrato you end up putting way too much pressure on the muscles under your chin. Those muscles are somewhat connected to the ones that move your larynx up and down. What I'm saying is, I don't want any pressure anywhere, but I especially don't want any pressure anywhere near the vocal cords. That's why I can't let you make vibrato by shaking your jaw.

Born with It

Some people think you have to be born with vibrato, but that's just not the case. All vibrato is manufactured.

When my daughter was three years old, we were watching the *Wizard of Oz*. When the Cowardly Lion sang "If I were king of the forest," I put the videotape on pause and imitated what the lion sounded like. "Forest," I sang, shaking my head up and down making a huge amount of vibrato. "Forest," she sang back to me, shaking her head and making the same silly, over-the-top vibrato I made. "That's called vibrato," I said to her. "Vibrato," she said. Two weeks later she was singing all of her songs around the house with the most beautiful vibrato I'd ever heard in my life. Before the *Wizard of Oz* there was no vibrato, afterward she had vibrato like a diva. All I needed to do was expose her to it and tell her that it was a good thing. She did the rest. From then on she listened and imitated the vibrato sounds of her favorite artists until she could sound like them.

If you already have a nice vibrato—great! If not, now's the perfect time for you to get one. Whether you learn it by imitating other singers when you're three years old or when you're thirty, everybody on the planet who has one made it for themselves. No one was ever just born with it.

Bigger Than You Think

In a minute when I give you your first exercise to find vibrato, I want you to remember something and put it in the back of your mind: *Vibrato is much bigger than you think.* It's not a tiny feeling somewhere in the throat. It's not a little wiggle that happens to bubble its way out without being noticed. It's a big thing you should feel in the very back part of your throat. The air bursts that make the vibrato happen are large, strong bursts of air that come flying out of the mouth, as big as a golf ball heading for the fairway. If your vibrato doesn't feel that big, you're probably not doing it right.

When I make vibrato I feel big air bursts hit the very back part of the roof of my mouth evenly. With that in mind, let's think about our breathing for a minute, and then move right along to our first vibrato exercise.

Remember Your Breathing

If you want great vibrato, you need to make sure that you're still doing the diaphragmatic breathing I taught you earlier. Let's review it:

1. Put your hand on your belly button.
2. Take a big breath in (through your nose) and pretend that you have a balloon in your stomach.
3. Fill up that balloon with air.
4. Exhale and let your stomach fall back in to its normal position.

When you're holding a note out trying to make vibrato, you have to make sure that your stomach is coming in the whole time you're singing out. The vibrato really needs that even airflow to help it along. If you try to make vibrato with your stomach tight and locked in one position, you're never going to get the vibrato to sound natural.

Vibrato Exercises

I call the first one the STOMACH PRESS.

Make a fist and place it right on top of your belly button, and then cover that fist with your other hand. Now say *"geeeeeeee,"* and as you do, push your hands in and out in an even pulsing motion. The goal is to send bursts of air to the back of your throat. As you do it, you should hear the straight and smooth *"geeeeeeee"* sound break into a vibratolike *"gee-ee-ee-ee."* Keep your hands moving in and out until you run out of breath, and then try it again. Pay attention to where you feel the air bursts are hitting the back part of your throat, right where the roof of your mouth meets the back of your tongue.

(PLEASE LISTEN TO MY DEMONSTRATION OF THE STOMACH PRESS ON TRACK 16 OF THE CD)

All I'm trying to do here is to show you how big vibrato should feel in your throat—it's not a small thing. Like I said above, it's bigger than you think. It takes a lot of air bursts to make it happen. Remember that in the beginning, it's tough to get the right speed of six beats per second, and you might feel like you're making phony, fake sounds in a completely unnatural way. It might be too fast or too slow, but keep playing with the speed of it. Once you get used to how and where it feels in the body, a little miracle happens. The voice begins to feel as though it's making vibrato on its own. When that happens, you'll be a very happy camper.

The next one is called the FINGER POINT.

Stand up and extend your favorite hand as though you were pointing at something. Keeping just your index finger out, pretend that you're shaking hands with someone. Move your hand up and down about ten inches and don't stop. As you do this, sing *"geeeeeeee"* and try to match the sound of your voice with the motion of your hand. It should come out in little bursts: *"gee-ee-ee-ee."*

Once again, concentrate on the back part of the roof of your mouth as you're making the sound. This is where you're trying to feel the bursts of air. Just follow along with the exercise on the CD and imitate me. Forget about sounding funny; just concentrate on making your voice move up and down like your hand and finger.

After you get pretty good at making an even vibrato sound while you're doing the FINGER POINT, you're ready to try the FINGER POINT PLUS.

Try doing this:

1. Take a nice big diaphragmatic breath and move your hand to the same position you did for the **FINGER POINT**.

2. Sing *"geeeeeeee"* like you did before and move your hand up and down in the same way.

3. After about three seconds, stop your hand from moving, but still try to keep the vibrato sound going.

This exercise is a little trickier. As soon as you stop your hand, the vibrato will probably last another second and then stop. But you can make it stay with a bit of practice. Concentrate on the air bursts hitting the back part of your throat; just don't think about your finger hand moving. It's not your hand that's making the vibrato happen anyway. You might think it is, but it's not. Your hand is simply sending a signal to your brain to make regular beats, and then the brain sends a message to the diaphragm and the vocal cords, and tells them to make it happen. The hand thing is just a key—it's not the engine of the car.

I believe it helps to visualize things. So think of vibrato as a series of mountains and valleys. We already learned how the air and vibrato travel in waves. So the mountain-valley idea goes perfectly with that. When more air is coming through, that's the mountain; when less air is coming out, that's the valley. With the

mountain-valley idea in your head, let's look at another exercise I call the AIR-TO-HAND RATIO:

1. Take a diaphragmatic breath and fill up your stomach area.
2. Place your fingers about three-quarters of an inch in front of your lips.
3. Sing the word *"geeeeeee"* and try to make the air pulse against your fingers.
4. Make a big breath of air hit your fingers, and then almost nothing: big-small, big-small, mountain-valley, mountain-valley.

Try to feel the big and small bursts of air hitting your fingers. Don't worry if your stomach is moving in and out a bit when you do this; we'll get rid of that later. Right now it's about making the vibrato sound, and getting close to the right speed of six beats per second.

Recap

Most audiences are not filled with vocal coaches and incredible musicians. Your average audience is made up of all kinds of people there just to be entertained and have a good time. There are certain sounds they recognize as good, and certain things they instantly know are bad. When you sing off pitch, the audience might not realize whether you're sharp or flat, but they'll know it's wrong and react negatively. Vibrato is a sound that people instantly recognize and associate with good singing. Vibrato is easy for the audience to hear, and in their minds it can quite often be the difference between a great singer and an amateur.

So keep practicing your vibrato until it feels natural. Remember, don't be impatient; it can take a while for that to happen. You could be stuck with the slow, funny-sounding vibrato for days, weeks, and even months before it speeds up and sounds amazing. Play with the exercises and make sure that you always come back to the CD and try to imitate the sounds you hear me make. That way you'll always be focused in the right direction.

LOVE NOTES
AND SONGS

chapter
FIVE

At my company in Los Angeles, Voiceplace, we're always looking to create new and exciting ways to enjoy singing. At the top of the list over the last few years, our goal was to invent a new form of sing-along, something that took the basic elements of karaoke but gave it a completely new twist. So after a year of development and two years of working to get the patent, "Love Notes" was born.

Love Notes is an amazing way to instantly sound more like the artists you love. All you have to do is follow along with four basic symbols, and do what they suggest. The symbols sit right above the lyrics and show you when to take a breath, when to get louder, when to add vibrato, and what voice to be in where. Each song is broken down into the four elements. The symbols are arranged for *you* to do exactly what the original artist did at that moment. Breath by breath, note by note, Love Notes will have you singing like your favorite superstar in no time.

The Symbols

The first symbol tells you when to take a breath, and it looks like this:

Breathe in

When you see this symbol, take a nice diaphragmatic breath. You remember how to do that:

1. Put your hand on your belly button.
2. Take a big breath in and pretend that you have a balloon in your stomach.
3. Fill up that balloon with air.
4. Exhale and let your stomach fall back in to its normal position.

The next symbol tells you when to add vibrato, and it looks like this:

ꟹꟹꟹꟹꟹ

Vibrato

Every time you see that symbol over a word or a part of a word, just add vibrato. If you're still having trouble making vibrato, it's OK for you to use the FINGER POINT helper I gave you in the chapter on vibrato. Later on when the vibrato becomes more natural, you can do it without the finger.

Next when you see a word or a part of a word in Love Notes that's in all capital letters, make it louder. It'll look just like this: The BIG words get LOUDER.

ALL CAPS
Louder

The last thing to watch for is the symbol that tells you when to be in chest, middle, or head voice, and it looks like this:

H head
M middle
C chest

You'll notice that Love Notes is divided into three main sections. Chest voice is the lower third, middle voice is the middle section, and head voice is the top portion. When the lyrics to the song are in the bottom area, just sing all of the words in chest voice. When any lyrics jump up to the middle section, you need to sing those words or parts of words in middle voice. If any of the notes of the song needs to go all the way to head voice, they'll be in the top area. If this sounds complicated, it's not. After a couple of minutes of trying the Love Notes system, you'll easily master it.

Most of the notes in popular music stay in the chest voice range anyway. So a lot of the words you'll be singing will be in the bottom area, chest voice. It'll be very easy to see when a word jumps out of the chest voice area and either goes to the middle or the head voice section.

Love Notes is very simple. Just follow along and look out for the symbols. The goal is not only to sound great, but to also have a great time while you're doing it.

Secrets

Aside from the symbols, when we start a new song, I'll give you one or more Love Notes secrets. These secrets will tell you more about the song and offer specific tips on how to sing it better. They will provide a road map, so you'll know what direction to go in, and hopefully never get lost.

The Songs

I've selected three megahit songs for us to learn and work with using the Love Notes. In order to do it, however, you'll need to be familiar with the songs first. Because we'll be singing from the lyrics only, without the music, you'll need to make sure that you know how the melody of each of the songs goes. I suggest that you either go to your own CD collection and find the original recordings, or go out and buy the CD and learn the songs. Once you have the melody down, you can then take full advantage of the Love Note symbols and secrets. Just play the song, sing, and do what the symbols tell you to do. After that, if you want to, you can sing the songs a capella, or maybe go out and get the karaoke versions so that you're the only one singing.

The three songs I've chosen for us to play with are:

1. "Beautiful," performed by Christina Aguilera
2. "U Got It Bad," performed by Usher
3. "Don't Know Why," performed by Norah Jones

So let's take a look at the song **"Beautiful,"** and figure out what to do with it. The Love Note symbols will show us when to use chest, middle, or head voice, where the vibrato goes, when to get louder, and where to take the breaths. But what else do we need to know about the song?

* ✳ Christina sings the verses of this song in a very breathy voice. It's OK for you to go ahead and try that too.
* ✳ As she gets into the chorus of the song, she moves out of that breathy sound into more of an edgy, brighter sound. Make sure that you imitate that also.
* ✳ Most of the song is sung in chest voice. In the first part of the song, there are a few little jumps up to middle, though:
* ✳ When she sings "Words can't bring me down," the "me" goes up to middle. Listen for that.
* ✳ Later the same thing happens when she sings "Words can't bring you down." The "you" also goes to middle voice.
* ✳ Later in the song when she sings "Everywhere we go," the word "everywhere" goes to middle voice.
* ✳ When she sings the words "The sun won't always shine," "always" and "shine" are definitely in middle voice.

**(PLEASE LISTEN TO MY DEMONSTRATION
OF SOME OF THE ABOVE ON TRACK 18 OF THE CD)**

love notes™

Beautiful

Breathe in
Go for a nice, relaxing diaphragmatic breath.

Vibrato
Add vibrato to that particular word.

ALL CAPS
Louder

Voices

H head
M middle
C chest

The symbols for chest, middle and head tell you which voice to be in where. You'll notice that each voice has its own individual line. When the words move to a different line, go to that voice.

Don't look at me

H

M

C Every DAY is so WONderFul

H

M

C And suddENLY, it's HARD to BREATHE

H

M

C NOW and THEN, I get INsecure

H

M

C From ALL the PAIN, I'm SO ASHAMED

H

M

C I AM BEAUTIFUL no MATTER WHAT they SAY

H

M ME

C WORDS CAN'T BRING DOWN

H

M

C I am BEAUTIFUL in EVERY SINGLE WAY

59 <<

love notes™

Breathe in
Go for a nice, relaxing diaphragmatic breath.

〰〰〰〰〰
Vibrato
Add vibrato to that particular word.

ALL CAPS
Louder

Voices

H head
M middle
C chest

The symbols for chest, middle and head tell you which voice to be in where. You'll notice that each voice has its own individual line. When the words move to a different line, go to that voice.

H
M   ME
C   Yes, WORDS can't BRING   DOWN

H
M
C   So don't you BRING me DOWN TODAY

H
M
C   Tell all your FRIENDS, YOU'RE DELIRIOUS

H
M
C   So consUMED in all YOUR DOOM

H
M
C   Trying hard to fill the EMPTiness

H
M
C   The PIECE is GONE and the puzzle UNdone

H
M
C   That's the WAY IT IS

love notes™

Breathe in
Go for a nice, relaxing diaphragmatic breath.

Vibrato
Add vibrato to that particular word.

ALL CAPS
Louder

Voices

H head
M middle
C chest

The symbols for chest, middle and head tell you which voice to be in where. You'll notice that each voice has its own individual line. When the words move to a different line, go to that voice.

H
M
C You are BEAUTIFUL no MATTER WHAT they SAY

H
M   YOU
C WORDS can't BRING   DOWN

H
M
C You are BEAUTIFUL in every SINgle WAY

H
M   YOU
C Yes, WORDS can't bring   DOWN

H
M
C Don't you BRING me DOWN TODAY

H
M
C No MATTER what we DO

H
M
C (no MATTER WHAT we DO)

love notes™

Breathe In
Go for a nice, relaxing diaphragmatic breath.

Vibrato
Add vibrato to that particular word.

ALL CAPS
Louder

Voices

H head
M middle
C chest

The symbols for chest, middle and head tell you which voice to be in where. You'll notice that each voice has its own individual line. When the words move to a different line, go to that voice.

No MATTER what we SAY

YEAH

(no MATTER what we SAY)

And EVERYWHERE we GO

(EVERYWHERE

we GO)

The SUN won't ALWAYS shine

ALWAYS SHINE)

(sun won't

they

We are BEAUTIFUL no MATTER what SAY

love notes™

Breathe in
Go for a nice, relaxing diaphragmatic breath.

〰〰〰〰〰
Vibrato
Add vibrato to that particular word.

ALL CAPS
Louder

Voices
Ⓗ head
Ⓜ middle
Ⓒ chest

The symbols for chest, middle and head tell you which voice to be in where. You'll notice that each voice has its own individual line. When the words move to a different line, go to that voice.

Ⓗ
Ⓜ us
Ⓒ Yes, WORDS WON'T BRING DOWN

Ⓗ
Ⓜ
Ⓒ We are BEAUTIFUL in EVERY SINGLE WAY

Ⓗ
Ⓜ us
Ⓒ Yes, WORDS CAN'T bring DOWN

Ⓗ
Ⓜ
Ⓒ Don't you BRING me DOWN today

Ⓗ
Ⓜ TODAY, YEAH
Ⓒ Don't you BRING me down

Ⓗ
Ⓜ
Ⓒ Don't you BRING me DOWN today

The next song is **"U Got It Bad,"** performed by Usher. He has a great voice, definitely worth imitating, and I especially like the way he uses vibrato. This song has plenty of notes that actually go up into the middle voice range. Here are some examples:

✳ In the first verse, when Usher sings "And everything in your past, you wanna let it go," "Let it" should go to middle voice. Even though a lot of you can hit those notes in chest voice, I still want you to try and go to middle.

✳ When Usher sings the words "Nobody wants to be alone, if you're touched by the words in this song," the words "be" and "words" should also go to middle voice.

✳ When you get to the chorus of the song, that's where you have one really high note. When Usher sings "If you miss a day without your friend your whole life's off track," the word "day" jumps way up into the middle voice. Based on the way he sings it, you might even want to make it sound a little more like head voice.

(PLEASE LISTEN TO MY DEMONSTRATION OF THE ABOVE ON TRACK 19 OF THE CD)

love notes™

Breathe in
Go for a nice, relaxing diaphragmatic breath.

〰〰〰
Vibrato
Add vibrato to that particular word.

ALL

DR

es

H head
M middle
C chest

The symbols for chest, middle and head tell you which voice to be in where. You'll notice that each voice has its own individual line. When the words move to a different line, go to that voice.

H
M Oh
C   no, no, no, no, no...

H
M
C When you feel it in your BODY

H
M
C You found someBODY who 〰 makes you CHANGE your

H
M
C WAYS

H
M
C Like hanging WITH your crew 〰

H
M
C Said you ACT like you're READY

H
M
C But you don't REALLY know 〰

love notes™

Breathe in
Go for a nice, relaxing diaphragmatic breath.

〜〜〜〜〜
Vibrato
Add vibrato to that particular word.

ALL CAPS
Louder

Voices

H head
M middle
C chest

The symbols for chest, middle and head tell you which voice to be in where. You'll notice that each voice has its own individual line. When the words move to a different line, go to that voice.

LET IT GO

And everyTHING in your PAST-you wanna

I've BEEN THERE, DONE it, messed around

After ALL THAT-this is what I FOUND

BE
NOBODY wants to   ALONE

WORDS
If you're TOUCHED by the   in this SONG

Then BABY...

U GOT IT, U GOT IT BAD

love notes™

Breathe in
Go for a nice, relaxing diaphragmatic breath.

Vibrato
Add vibrato to that particular word.

ALL CAPS
Louder

Voices
- H head
- M middle
- C chest

The symbols for chest, middle and head tell you which voice to be in where. You'll notice that each voice has its own individual line. When the words move to a different line, go to that voice.

When you're ON THE PHONE

HANG up and you CALL RIGHT BACK

U GOT IT, U GOT IT BAD

DAY
If you MISS a   without your FRIEND

Your whole LIFE'S OFF TRACK

You KNOW you got it BAD when you're STUCK

in the HOUSE

love notes™

Breathe in
Go for a nice, relaxing diaphragmatic breath.

Vibrato
Add vibrato to that particular word.

ALL CAPS
Louder

Voices

H head
M middle
C chest

The symbols for chest, middle and head tell you which voice to be in where. You'll notice that each voice has its own individual line. When the words move to a different line, go to that voice.

C You don't WANNA HAVE FUN

C It's ALL you think ABOUT

C U got it BAD when you're OUT with SOMEONE

C But you KEEP on THINKin' bout SOMEBODY ELSE

C U got it BAD

M SAY
C When you   that you LOVE 'em

C And you REALLY know

love notes™

Breathe in
Go for a nice, relaxing diaphragmatic breath.

〜〜〜〜〜〜
Vibrato
Add vibrato to that particular word.

ALL CAPS
Louder

Voices

H	head
M	middle
C	chest

The symbols for chest, middle and head tell you which voice to be in where. You'll notice that each voice has its own individual line. When the words move to a different line, go to that voice.

(H)
(M)
(C) EVERYTHING that used to MATTER, don't MATTER

(H)
(M)
(C) no more ↓

(H)
(M)
(C) Like my MONEY, ↓ all my CARS ↓

(H)
(M)
(C) (You can have it all back) ↓

(H)
(M) CANDY ↓
(C) Flowers, cards and

(H)
(M)
(C) (I do it just cause I'm...) ↓

(H)
(M)
(C) Said I'm FORTUNATE to HAVE YOU GIRL ↓

love notes™

Breathe in
Go for a nice, relaxing diaphragmatic breath.

Vibrato
Add vibrato to that particular word.

ALL CAPS
Louder

Voices

H head
M middle
C chest

The symbols for chest, middle and head tell you which voice to be in where. You'll notice that each voice has its own individual line. When the words move to a different line, go to that voice.

I WANT you to KNOW

I REALLY ADORE YOU

All my PEOPLE who KNOW what's going ON

LOOK at your MATE, help me SING MY SONG

Tell her I'M YOUR man, YOU'RE MY girl

WHOLE WIDE WORLD
I'm gonna TELL IT to the

Ladies say I'M YOUR girl, YOU'RE MY MAN

love notes™

U Got It Bad

Breathe in
Go for a nice, relaxing diaphragmatic breath.

Vibrato
Add vibrato to that particular word.

ALL CAPS
Louder

Voices

- (H) head
- (M) middle
- (C) chest

The symbols for chest, middle and head tell you which voice to be in where. You'll notice that each voice has its own individual line. When the words move to a different line, go to that voice.

(H)
(M) BEST I CAN
(C) Promise to LOVE you the

(H)
(M)
(C) See I've BEEN THERE, DONE IT, messed around

(H)
(M)
(C) After ALL THAT–THIS is what I found

(H)
(M) JUST LIKE ME
(C) EveryONE of y'all are

(H)
(M)
(C) It's too BAD that YOU CAN'T SEE

(H)
(M) BAD... HEY
(C) That you got it

(H)
(M)
(C) U GOT IT, U GOT IT BAD

love notes™

Breathe in
Go for a nice, relaxing diaphragmatic breath.

Vibrato
Add vibrato to that particular word.

ALL CAPS
Louder

Voices

H head
M middle
C chest

The symbols for chest, middle and head tell you which voice to be in where. You'll notice that each voice has its own individual line. When the words move to a different line, go to that voice.

(H)
(M)
(C) When you're ON THE PHONE

(H)
(M)
(C) HANG up and you CALL RIGHT BACK

(H)
(M)
(C) U GOT IT, U GOT IT BAD

(H)
(M) DAY
(C) If you miss a without your FRIEND

(H)
(M)
(C) Your whole LIFE'S OFF TRACK

(H)
(M)
(C) You KNOW you got it BAD when you're STUCK

(H)
(M)
(C) in the HOUSE

love notes™

Breathe in
Go for a nice, relaxing diaphragmatic breath.

〰〰〰〰
Vibrato
Add vibrato to that particular word.

ALL CAPS
Louder

Voices

H head
M middle
C chest

The symbols for chest, middle and head tell you which voice to be in where. You'll notice that each voice has its own individual line. When the words move to a different line, go to that voice.

H
M
C You don't WANNA HAVE FUN

H
M
C It's ALL you think ABOUT

H
M
C U got it BAD when you're OUT with someONE

H
M
C But you KEEP on THINKin' bout SOMEBODY ELSE

H
M
C U got it bad

H
M
C U GOT IT, U GOT IT BAD

H
M
C When you're ON THE PHONE

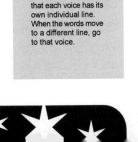

73 <<

love notes™

Breathe in
Go for a nice, relaxing diaphragmatic breath.

Vibrato
Add vibrato to that particular word.

ALL CAPS
Louder

Voices

(H) head
(M) middle
(C) chest

The symbols for chest, middle and head tell you which voice to be in where. You'll notice that each voice has its own individual line. When the words move to a different line, go to that voice.

U Got It Bad

(H)
(M)
(C) HANG up and you CALL RIGHT BACK

(H)
(M)
(C) U GOT IT, U GOT IT BAD

(H)
(M) DAY
(C) If you miss a   without your FRIEND

(H)
(M)
(C) Your whole LIFE'S OFF TRACK

(H)
(M)
(C) You KNOW you got it BAD when you're STUCK

(H)
(M)
(C) in the HOUSE

(H)
(M)
(C) You don't WANNA HAVE FUN

>> **74**

love notes™

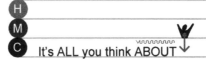

Breathe in
Go for a nice, relaxing diaphragmatic breath.

Vibrato
Add vibrato to that particular word.

ALL CAPS
Louder

Voices

H head
M middle
C chest

The symbols for chest, middle and head tell you which voice to be in where. You'll notice that each voice has its own individual line. When the words move to a different line, go to that voice.

H
M
C It's ALL you think ABOUT

H
M
C U got it BAD when you're OUT with someONE

H
M
C But you KEEP on THINKin' bout SOMEBODY ELSE

H
M
C U GOT IT BAD

The next song is **"Don't Know Why,"** performed by Norah Jones. I think she has a beautiful voice. I find it soothing and easy to listen to. It doesn't hit me over the head with brassy, edgy sounds that force me to listen. It gently asks me to pull up a comfortable chair, have a cup of tea (without caffeine), and relax. Here are some tips to help you sing it:

* Notice that when Norah sings a riff (a small cluster of notes), she sounds completely different from a singer like Christina Aguilera. For example, when Norah sings the words "On my mind," she plays around with the word "my" by separating it into a few very simple notes. She also moves slowly from note to note, which makes it a lot easier to sing along with her. Listen to her CD and you'll hear what I mean. When Christina sings a riff she uses a much more complicated pattern of notes, and she sings them very fast. That makes it extra hard to sing along with her.

* When Norah sings the verses of the song, she has a lovely breathy quality to her voice, enough to be interesting without making the vocal cords dry and swollen. But when you listen to her go higher into the middle voice range, she gets really clear and strong, and that's exactly what I want you to do.

* When you listen to Norah sing, you'll notice that she has a wonderful control of volume. She is very even all the way up and down the range. When you sing the song, try to keep a level, constant volume going throughout.

* Notice also that Norah slides from note to note quite often. It's an interesting little style thing. I don't want you to do that all the time—you'll sound like a drunken sailor—but it's a good idea for you to imitate her and learn to use it sometimes.

* This song has a number of parts that go up into the middle voice range. Here are some examples:

✶ When Norah sings "My heart is drenched in wine," "the words "heart" and "is" should go to middle voice.

✶ When she sings the words "You'll be on my mind forever," the words "you'll," "be," and "on" should also go to middle voice.

(PLEASE LISTEN TO MY DEMONSTRATION
OF THE ABOVE ON TRACK 20 OF THE CD)

love notes™

Breathe in
Go for a nice, relaxing diaphragmatic breath.

Vibrato
Add vibrato to that particular word.

ALL CAPS
Louder

Voices

H head
M middle
C chest

The symbols for chest, middle and head tell you which voice to be in where. You'll notice that each voice has its own individual line. When the words move to a different line, go to that voice.

H
M
C I WAITED 'til I saw the SUN

H
M
C I don't know WHY I DIDN'T COME

H
M
C I LEFT you BY the HOUSE of FUN

H
M
C I don't know WHY I DIDN'T COME

H
M
C I don't know WHY I DIDN'T COME

H
M
C WHEN I SAW the BREAK of day

H
M
C I wished that I COULD fly AWAY

love notes™

Breathe in
Go for a nice, relaxing diaphragmatic breath.

Vibrato
Add vibrato to that particular word.

ALL CAPS
Louder

Voices

H head
M middle
C chest

The symbols for chest, middle and head tell you which voice to be in where. You'll notice that each voice has its own individual line. When the words move to a different line, go to that voice.

H
M
C InSTEAD of KNEEling IN the SAND

H
M
C CATCHING TEARdrops IN MY hand

H
M HEART IS
C My DRENCHED IN WINE

H
M YOU'LL BE
C But ON MY MIND

H
M
C ForEVER

H
M
C OUT across the ENDLESS sea

H
M
C I would DIE in ECSTASY

love notes™

Breathe in
Go for a nice, relaxing diaphragmatic breath.

Vibrato
Add vibrato to that particular word.

ALL CAPS
Louder

Voices

(H) head
(M) middle
(C) chest

The symbols for chest, middle and head tell you which voice to be in where. You'll notice that each voice has its own individual line. When the words move to a different line, go to that voice.

BUT I'll be a BAG of BONES

Driving DOWN the ROAD ALONE

HEART IS
My   DRENCHED IN WINE

YOU'LL BE ON
But   MY MIND

FOREVER

SOMEthing has to MAKE you run

I don't know WHY I didn't COME

love notes™

Breathe in
Go for a nice, relaxing diaphragmatic breath.

Vibrato
Add vibrato to that particular word.

ALL CAPS
Louder

Voices

H head
M middle
C chest

The symbols for chest, middle and head tell you which voice to be in where. You'll notice that each voice has its own individual line. When the words move to a different line, go to that voice.

FINDING YOUR ORIGINAL STYLE

chapter SIX

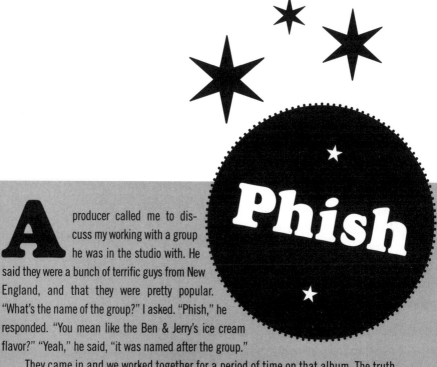

Phish

A producer called me to discuss my working with a group he was in the studio with. He said they were a bunch of terrific guys from New England, and that they were pretty popular. "What's the name of the group?" I asked. "Phish," he responded. "You mean like the Ben & Jerry's ice cream flavor?" "Yeah," he said, "it was named after the group."

They came in and we worked together for a period of time on that album. The truth is, in the beginning, I really wasn't familiar at all with who they were and what they were all about. I had no idea that these guys were the new Grateful Dead. It was a bit shocking to find out later just how popular they were. To me, it was just a bunch of nice guys and some interesting music. I remember one day we worked on a particular song they were going to record. The song wasn't in English, however; it was in Hebrew. "What makes you think the general public wants to hear a song in Hebrew?" I asked naively. "We think it's cool," they answered.

The reason I bring this story up at all is to talk about original style. Phish wasn't interested in what the public wanted, they were only interested in creating and playing the kind of music they loved. They would get on stage and play and sing their hearts out. If the audience liked the songs, that was cool. If not, they were still going to follow their own path. That's a good lesson to learn about originality. It's not always about pleasing someone else—it's about creating something that you believe in.

✳ ✳ ✳ ✳ ✳ ✳ ✳ ✳ ✳ ✳ ✳ ✳ ✳ ✳ ✳ ✳ ✳ ✳ ✳

Celebrity Tidbit

I asked superstar **Cher** if there was one piece of advice she would give to someone who wants to be a singer, and here's what she said:

If you truly have the talent and the drive to succeed, put your head down and put one foot in front of the other. Remember it is a complete constant commitment!

I think her words are 100 percent true. If you really believe that you have what it takes to be a great singer, you need to keep walking one step at a time toward your goal. No matter what happens to slow you down, or what obstacle presents itself, you need to have faith and total commitment.

✳ ✳ ✳ ✳ ✳ ✳ ✳ ✳ ✳ ✳ ✳ ✳ ✳ ✳ ✳ ✳ ✳ ✳ ✳

Everybody's Different

Did you ever notice that everyone's speaking voice sounds different? When a friend calls you on the phone you recognize his or her voice right away. Well, being a great singer is all about sounding unique too. Like a great painting, your voice will need to exude originality and uniqueness, and show everyone else just how special you are—that you are truly one of a kind.

I've spent years developing a way to help singers find originality. And the funny thing is, it all starts with the ability to imitate. If you ever really want to sound like *yourself* you first need to learn how to sound like *somebody else*. As funny as that sounds, you can't even begin to create a unique sound until you can mimic what other singers are doing. In order to do that, you need to learn the following steps:

Step 1—Listen to Great Singers

Sounds easy enough, right? But when I say listen, I mean really pay attention to every little sound the singer makes. Not just the verses and the choruses of the song, but the singer's every vowel, consonant, turn, cry, swoop, and jump. I want you to pretend that you're in biology class and you have to dissect a voice instead of a frog.

When a singer gets airy like Norah Jones singing the words "Don't know why I didn't come," I want you to notice.

When a singer gets louder, like Avril Lavigne singing "It's a damn cold night," I want you to notice.

When a singer gets bassy like Tony Braxton singing "Unbreak my heart," I want you to be aware of it.

When Madonna gets nasal singing "Like a virgin," I want you to take note of it.

When Faith Hill sings "That's the way that love's supposed to be," I want you to realize that on the word "supposed" she went into her middle voice.

If you listen carefully, I know that you'll begin to hear all kinds of things going on that you can recognize and make note of.

Pick a Song

Pick a singer and a specific song that you love from your CD collection. Choose an artist that you really admire and wish you could sound like.

Get out a pencil and paper, listen carefully to the song, and write down the lyrics. I want you to have them right in front of you as you listen to the CD. Seeing the lyrics makes it easier to focus just on the singer instead of wondering what the words are.

I also recommend listening to the music with headphones. It helps you hear everything in a bit more detail. But remember to only use the headphones when you are listening to the original artist. Every time that you *sing* you should *not* use the headphones.

With the completed lyric sheet in hand, sit down in front of the CD player and make sure that you can reach the pause and rewind buttons.

1. **Play the first part of the song (about thirty seconds of singing) and listen to what the singer does. Pay attention to when the singer gets louder or softer. Pay attention to when the voice gets airy, or edgy, or gravelly, or**

bassy, or nasal. Replay the song and listen again. Do this over and over until you really feel like you have it memorized.

2. Now start the song from the beginning again but this time let it play for about a minute longer (the first verse, chorus, second verse, and second chorus). Replay it again and again until you feel you really know what the singer sounds like.

3. Then go back to the beginning of the song and play it all the way through until the end. Keep focusing on every sound the singer makes.

You might be thinking, I'm not a voice teacher, and I can't hear all of the little things going on when someone sings! To that I say, that with a little bit of practice, you can easily hear the things you need to hear.

Step 2—Sing-Along

Now that you're familiar with the song, I want you to take the headphones off, play the song again, and start to sing along. When you do so, you need to pretend that you and the artist are like Siamese twins joined at the throat. Don't sing it like *you;* try to sound exactly like the *artist.* Right now it doesn't matter what you normally sing like. It only matters that you can make your voice do what the other singer is doing.

With the lyric sheet in hand, and your finger near the pause and rewind buttons:

1. Play the first thirty seconds or so of the song and sing along with the artist. Replay it and sing it again. Do this over and over until you really feel like you have it down.

2. Now start it from the beginning again and let the CD play for about a minute longer (the first verse, chorus, second verse, and second chorus). Replay it again and again until you feel like you and the singer are sharing the same DNA molecules.

3. Then go to the beginning of the song and sing it all the way through until the end. Keep focusing on every sound that you and the singer make together.

Celebrity Tidbit

brian McKNIGHT

I asked superstar **Brian McKnight** if he had any advice for someone who was trying to find their own original style, and here's what he said:

Find things in people's voices that you really like and put those elements together and develop your style. Finding your style is the hardest thing to do as a singer.

That's exactly what I'm teaching you in this chapter. There's nothing new, just new combinations of sounds that we've heard before. When you put those sounds together in your new voice, you can create magic.

Step 3—Sing-Along and Record Yourself

Now I want you to set up a tape recorder so that you can not only play the song you've been working on, but can also record yourself singing along with it. It doesn't have to be anything fancy or expensive. A portable recorder will be fine, as long as you can hear what you really sound like when you play the recording back. You can even use a karaoke machine if you have one.

With the lyric sheet in hand, and your finger on the pause and rewind buttons:

1. **Play the first part of the song, sing along with the artist, and record it. Then listen back to the recording you just made. Do you sound like the other singer? Do some parts sound similar and other parts don't? No problem.**

2. **Just rewind the tape and sing it and record yourself over again. Do this little by little until you feel like you can sing the whole song sounding as much like the original artist as possible. Keep working until you feel like you and the artist really sound alike.**

Step 4—Lose the Music and Sing A Capella

Now I want you to turn the CD off and sing the song "a capella" (with no music). Make sure that you're still recording yourself. After you sing, go back and listen to your recording. Without the artist singing with you, do you still sound like the original vacalist? If you do, *great!* If you don't, *no problem!* Simply go back one step (to Step 3) and try singing and recording again with the original artist. Then try Step 4 again and see how you sound.

Step 5—Sing a Different Song

Now that you've gotten good at imitating one artist singing one particular song, we need to try your impersonation skills out on a different song.

Think of another song that you love, sung by a different artist. Now try to sing the new song sounding just like the first singer. For example, let's say you picked "Genie in a Bottle" by Christina Aguilera for the first artist and song you were trying to imitate. Now you should pick a song like Pink's "Just Like a Pill" and try to sing it exactly like Christina would. That is, try to imagine and make all of the sounds that Christina would make if she were singing "Just Like a Pill."

I suggest you start out by recording yourself a capella singing the new song. If you just put on the CD with Pink singing, you would most probably forget all of the Christina sounds you just worked so hard to get.

Later, after you get good at doing it without the music, maybe you can find a karaoke version of the second song and try to sing along with the track.

Remember, any time you don't think you sound like the singer you're working on, *go back one step.* This whole process can take a few days or a few weeks. Eventually, if you work on it, I promise that you'll be able to do it.

Putting It All Together

OK, so you've gotten really good at singing like Christina Aguilera or whoever else you picked as your first singer to imitate. Now what do you do? You don't have original style yet. Guess what? Now it's time to pick another singer to imitate, and start the steps out again from the beginning. If you love to sing, this is not bad news. Singing isn't work, it's fun, and remember that at the end of the rainbow you'll end up sounding original, unique, and incredible.

Just so you get a total picture of what I want you to do, I'm going to ask you to get good at imitating about ten singers. I want you to go through all of the above steps with ten singers that you love. And don't pick singers that sound exactly alike. Try to mix it up a bit. Find one singer who sounds great on the low notes, such as Tony Braxton, and work on owning those sounds. Then pick a singer who sounds great on the high notes, such as Celine Dion, and imitate her for a while. Go for a big assortment of singers and different sounds.

✴ ✴

Celebrity Tidbit

I asked superstar **Nelly** how to find an original style, and here's what he said:

Yeah, try and find it! We're from the Midwest, and so we have tried to show people what the Midwest and St. Louis is all about, so our style is unique to us. We don't sound like other groups from the West or the East Coast, or like the fellas from the Dirty South. If you got something you believe in, then go with it, even if it doesn't sound like the rest. That's what will set you apart.

✴ ✴

One day a recording artist student of mine named Rhapsody came into my office frustrated with the progress she was making. She was working diligently on the same steps to originality that I've given you here. She would study Whitney Houston and then go to a recording session a few days later and the producer would say, "You sound too much like Whitney Houston." Over the next week at home she would work on Aretha Franklin and then a few days later go back into the recording studio, only to have the producer say, "Now you sound too much like Aretha Franklin." She was understandably upset.

So do you know what I told her? I complimented her on being such a great student and really working on her skills to imitate other singers. But I told her the time had come to test all of her hard work. I challenged her to go back into the studio and forget about originality and style. I promised her that when the time was right, originality would just pour out of her. She had already done all the homework. She could easily sound like at least ten great singers. Now all she needed was for those sounds to combine inside of her and come out as a completely "new" voice.

A few days later she went into the studio and decided to sing with no style. She was sick and tired of sounding like other singers and was ready to just admit that she couldn't be original. She started to sing and gave absolutely no thought to style or originality. She didn't try to sound like any of the singers she loved. She just let it out plain and simple with no frills. When she finished that take, she expected the producer to tell her to go home and pick a new job from the want ads. Instead he said, "That was the best you've ever sounded." He said that he'd never heard her sing with such style and originality before. *She was in shock.* So what had happened? Well, it all just came together at that moment. All of the sounds she had been studying suddenly melded into a sound that was really *her.* From that day on she was confident that she was a great singer with real style.

In the end, just like Rhapsody learned, it's all about creating the perfect recipe using the ingredients you have at your disposal. Think of yourself as a great chef-to-be. You go into the kitchen and try to make an amazing dish with the ingredients you have in the fridge and the cupboard. A little of this, a bit of that, stir it up, cook it for a while, put it on a beautiful plate, and serve it to people who love it and want more. Style and originality are just like that. By the time you've mastered the imitation of the ten singers you picked, you'll own this completely new library of sounds that you didn't have before you started the journey.

At first when you sing songs you'll sound like "this" singer here and "that" singer there, and maybe you'll feel like you have some kind of multiple personality syndrome. The good news is, after some time, all of those voices will blend together and become something unique: the new you. It can take a week, a month, or a year; it's hard to say. But if you keep playing with the new sounds you'll find the pot of gold at the end of the rainbow.

Original Songs

A lot of times it's easier to find an original style if you have original music to sing. I believe that all of us have the ability to write. Some people are better with lyrics, some with melodies, but everyone who wants to be a singer should at least try to write something. Who knows, maybe you'll end up writing your first big hit song. Take a class, read books, study the music you love, and try to create something. What's the worst thing that can happen? Your songs will all be bad and you'll never show them to anyone anyway.

Singing an original song gives you a blank slate to create whatever sounds you imagine. You don't have anyone to copy; you only have yourself and your ideas to lean on. Though this might sound scary, it can also challenge you to be more confident and unique.

OVERCOMING STAGE FRIGHT

chapter SEVEN

You love to sing. Alone in your bedroom you sing and dance around the room like a platinum-selling superstar. Then your mom comes in and suddenly you clam up like a safe with a lost combination lock. She begs you to come into the living room and entertain her friends, but that totally freaks you out.

The thought of performing in front of people makes you way too nervous, and so you just avoid the whole idea. But think about it: How are you going to become the next Avril Lavigne, or Michelle Branch, or John Mayer, if you can't sing in front of people?

What you need to know is, just about every "famous" singer used to feel exactly the same way you do now about performing in public. But they did something about it: They eventually got over it. They leaned to accept the feelings and let nothing stop them.

✳ ✳ ✳ ✳ ✳ ✳ ✳ ✳ ✳ ✳ ✳ ✳ ✳ ✳ ✳ ✳ ✳ ✳ ✳ ✳

Celebrity Tidbit

I asked superstar **Nelly** if he gets stage fright, and if he still gets nervous singing in front of a live audience, and here's what he said:

No, not anymore. After the past two years, we have performed in front of so many people, we're cool with it. At first, yeah, I was nervous, but it was cool because I had the ticks on stage with me.

The key is just to block out the crowd and just let it flow. Sometimes I feel like I'm in my own world when I'm on stage.

Thank goodness that over time it gets easier to sing in front of people. Nelly is right on target when he talks about learning how to close out the noise and create his own private world on stage. It's so easy to get distracted and lose your focus.

Great performers are like a giant lightbulb. The switch gets flipped, they light up themselves, and then they light up the whole audience.

It's a Good Thing

Eventually every performer realizes that once you get past the stage-fright thing, being on stage singing to an audience who loves you and your music is an amazing thing. It's an incredibly life-changing experience that should never be missed if possible.

So the good news is, singing in public doesn't have to scare you to death. I'll show you how to turn your nervousness into positive energy that'll guarantee a great performance every time. And whether you're singing to one person or a hundred, you'll be ready.

And when I say stage fright, I don't mean that there has to actually be a stage involved. You could be singing in your bedroom, living room, on a street corner, or in front of thousands of fans screaming your name.

My goal in this chapter is to convince you that stage fright is actually a *good* thing. It's the body getting you ready to do something special, giving you moments of superhuman strength, trying to help you achieve incredible results in difficult situations.

But to understand about stage fright you need to know a little bit about your own autonomic nervous system.

Fight or Flight

Let's say you're walking home from school and you decide to take a quick shortcut through an alley you've never been down before. Suddenly a very loud noise scares the heck out of you. You feel a big rush of blood to your head as if you were going to faint. But instead of fainting, you run like the wind right out of the alley. You had no idea your little feet could even move that fast, but there you are, out of the alley and out of danger. If this was a fifty-yard dash for the Olympics, you would have just won a gold medal. That was the autonomic nervous system in action.

When you get in a potentially dangerous situation, the autonomic nervous system kicks in and gives you a boost of energy to help you get away from the danger.

Have you ever heard stories of parents lifting up cars for a few seconds to get their kids out from underneath? That's the autonomic nervous system at work.

Stage fright is basically a "good" thing with a "bad" name. Somehow over the years, it just ended up getting a bad rap. In truth, it's just the body getting you ready to do something bigger, stronger, faster, and more special than you normally do. It's an amazing gift of extra energy, and you should start thinking of it like that.

Let me tell you the story of two superstars who shared the same exact feelings of stage fright, and yet how amazingly different each situation turned out.

streisand AND SPRINGSTEEN

Backstage with Barbra Streisand . . . she's feeling really nervous. Her hands are sweating, her stomach is in knots, and she feels like throwing up. All she can think of is, I hate performing live, why do I put myself through this?

Backstage with Bruce Springsteen . . . he's feeling very nervous. His hands are clammy, his pulse is racing, and he feels like vomiting. He's thinking, Now I'm ready for the stage. The fans are out there and I'm ready to give them the show of their lives. I'm the Boss!

Both superstars had the exact same symptoms before performing, and yet only Bruce turned it into a positive thing.

* * * * * * * * * * * * * * * * * * * *

Celebrity Tidbit

I asked superstar **Luther Vandross** whether he still gets stage fright, and here's what he said:

Stage fright comes and goes. On tour, I feel most secure. When it's a one-shot TV appearance in an air-conditioned studio, I worry.

I think Luther is expressing exactly what most performers feel: Stage fright does come and go. You learn to live with it and try to make the most out of every situation. It's humbling to hear that someone as phenomenal a singer as Luther still gets nervous sometimes. He says that he'd rather be on stage with thousands of people than in a little room with a TV camera. I totally understand. On stage he gets all the energy and love from the fans, which is why performing live can be such a high. But no matter how nice the TV cameraman is, he's just not going to give off the same kind of energy.

* * * * * * * * * * * * * * * * * * * *

Butterflies

Do you remember the last time you had a date with someone you really liked? Can you think back to the week before the date? Do you remember what you were thinking and feeling?

Maybe you were thinking things like: I wonder where we should go? How will the evening turn out? I wonder if I'll get a good-night kiss?

Can you remember driving to the house to pick your date up, or hearing a car that was there to pick you up? Do you remember the feelings you had in your stomach? Did you feel like butterflies were jumping around in there uncontrollably? Do you remember liking that feeling?

The fact is, when it comes to butterflies in the tummy, most of us would agree that it's a positive thing. The excitement you feel right before an amazing date or a special event is a total rush, a very good thing.

So, what's the difference between stage fright and butterflies? *There isn't any difference.*

Realizing that, we need to stop looking at the nervous feelings that happen before we sing in public as a bad thing. Those feelings are there to help us, not to get in the way.

Breathing by the Numbers

Even though stage fright can actually be a positive thing, sometimes the nervous feelings hit you so suddenly that you could use a minute or two to calm down a bit. For that very situation, I want to offer you a breathing exercise to help you relax a little and catch your breath. Then you can focus on the positive side of the extra energy coming your way. I call it BREATHING BY THE NUMBERS:

1. **Take a big breath in through your nose.**
2. **Fill up your stomach as if you had a big balloon in there.**
3. **As you exhale, let your stomach fall back to its normal position and count slowly out loud from 1 to 10.**
4. **Go back and keep practicing steps 1, 2, and 3 until you feel a lot more calm and centered.**

This exercise will really help you to slow down and regulate your breathing when the nervousness suddenly pushes your pedal to the metal.

* *

Celebrity Tidbit

brian McKNIGHT

I asked superstar **Brian McKnight** about stage fright, and here's what he said:

I have never had stage fright. Never! I believe an audience is like a shark, and fright is like blood in the water.

I love that quote. I agree that the audience will totally focus on your fear if you expose it to them. If you keep focusing on the positive, you have nothing to worry about.

* *

Too Prepared to Be Scared

I want to give you some other good advice about stage fright. One of the reasons you're *scared* is because you're really not *prepared*. I remember when I was working with the Jacksons on a huge tour. Michael used to practice his vocal exercises four hours a day. I know that sounds crazy, but he'd heard that Pavarotti, the great opera star, practiced his vocal warm-ups four hours a day, and he figured that whatever was good enough for Pavarotti was good enough for Michael. Aside from the four hours of just doing voice exercises, Michael also had a very extensive rehearsal schedule. The lighting, the effects, and the choreography were so elaborate that they required a great deal of practice. There were hundreds of cues where the music did a specific thing, the lights did a specific thing, and Michael and his brothers had to also be doing a very specific thing at that very second. If Michael was two feet to the left or three seconds late, it could mess up everything. So hours and hours of rehearsal time went into making sure that everybody would do exactly what they were supposed to do every minute of the show. When Michael went for the moonwalk and sang a particular phrase, he was confident that after a ton of practice he really had it down. He wasn't nervous because he had done it right thousands of times before in rehearsal and in performance.

So let's be honest: One of the main reasons you get nervous is that you're still not as good as you could be. You haven't practiced your voice enough, or the song enough, or your moves enough. You can't guarantee that something won't go wrong because, you haven't really fixed all of the problems yet.

If *you* love it in rehearsal, the audience will probably love it in performance.

But, if you're still only so-so, and you're supposed to be your greatest fan, then you probably have every reason to be nervous. *Singing is fun.* Singing well and performing in front of people who love you is even *more fun!*

Superstar performers may have been born with extra talent, but it's practice, practice, and more practice that makes it all work out in the end. So do whatever you need to get ready for singing in public.

When that audience is standing on their feet clapping and cheering for you, all the hard work will be more than worth it. You'll feel like you hung the moon and set the stars in the skies!

Recap

I hope that this chapter has convinced you to at least try to look at stage fright as a positive thing. When you start to get nervous, realize that your body is doing everything it can to help you out.

When your pulse is racing, that's a good thing. When you feel those butterflies in the stomach, that's a good thing!

You're not getting ready to take a nap. Your fans are out there waiting for the show of their lives, and you *can* give it to them.

Remember: *You love to sing!*

Get out there and have the time of your life.

THE PERFECT DIET

chapter EIGHT

Did your mom ever give you tea with honey and lemon? As much as she loves you and was trying to do the right thing, she never knew that the caffeine and the honey was giving you extra thick phlegm in your throat, and that's a bad thing. And because the tea was hot, it was also making your vocal cords freak out. I'll show you just what to eat and drink to have a killer body and voice.

Now, when it comes to a singer's diet, there's really only one place to start: *Water, water,* and more *water.* Knowing that the vocal cords are rubbing up against each other hundreds to thousands of times per second, it shouldn't surprise anybody that they get dry.

What if I asked you to start rubbing your hands together for hours and hours every day? And by the way, while you're rubbing, I also want you to blow on them. What do you think would happen?

First, your hands would start to get red and swollen, and then you would most probably develop calluses, extra hard layers of skin. You would soon have to give up on your secret fantasy of becoming a hand model, and within no time at all your hands would look more like those of a ditch digger who had worked twenty-four-hour straight shifts for the last ten years.

That's similar to what happens with your vocal cords. When they don't get the moisture they need, they get red and swollen and can develop calluses, called nodules or nodes. Believe me, you don't want that to happen. If it does, and vocal therapy and rest don't fix it, you're looking at surgery. That's right: hospital, surgeon, knife, recovery—the whole rotten egg.

How does that extra few glasses of water sound now? Not that bad, right?

* *

Celebrity Tidbit

I asked superstar **Nelly** about diet, and here's what he said:

I don't do much before my shows except try to drink a lot of water to loosen up my throat. I am a vegetarian, and so I don't eat any meat, fish, or chicken. Sometimes I will drink hot tea if I feel my throat tightening up. Remember, though, rapping and singing are a little different. I don't need to hit the high notes.

I'm really impressed by his diet. Here's a guy who's committed to eating healthy foods. And his advice on water is perfect. He knows what you should know: Water can fix just about everything in the voice.

* *

A Gallon

The best singers' diet starts with—hold on to your hats—at least a half-gallon of water a day, and I recommend trying to drink even more than that, as much as a gallon.

There aren't that many bathrooms in the house, you might be saying to yourself. To which I reply, I don't think you'll really mind going to the rest room a few more times a day, as long as it helps you to sing like a superstar.

Why so much water? The reason is this: When you drink water, your bloodstream first sends it to all of the vital organs in the body: the heart, brain, and so on. The vital organs need it the most, and staying alive is always a good idea.

At the very end of the water line, pretty much after every other body part gets the water it needs, are the salivary glands: the system that produces phlegm, the mucus of the throat. If there happens to be any water left over, they might get some. But being at the end of the line doesn't always guarantee them all the water they need to do a good job. That's why we need to drink at least a half-gallon of water every day. When you do that, the salivary glands make nice watery phlegm that coats and lubricates the vocal cords and keeps them happy.

When your vocal cords are happy and healthy, great singing is a whole lot easier to achieve.

By the way, when I say water, I don't mean the water that's in your coffee, tea, lemonade, or soda. I mean plain, pure water. Once you mix it up with other things, you open up a whole new can of worms that we still need to talk about.

Coffee and Tea

Let's say that I got you a job to be a hand model, and the photo shoot is at 3:00 P.M. today. What if you decided to take a very hot bath at 2:00? After soaking for about thirty minutes, you would get out and take a look at your hands. What would they look like? Would they be beautiful and ready to be photographed? *No way.* They would probably look more like prunes. The reason for that is that the temperature of liquids affects the size of tissues. Not Kleenex—I'm talking about the muscles and tissues that are part of the vocal cords. When you drink anything that's too hot or even too cold, the size of the tissues can change—and that's not a good thing for singing.

Earlier in the book I mentioned that there were two holes in the back part of the throat—one for food and liquid, and one for air—and that the vocal cords live down in the air hole. So when you drink, the coffee or tea or whatever goes down the food and liquid hole, not down where the vocal cords live. Still, even though the hot or cold drink doesn't touch the cords, they're still affected by the extreme temperature, because it magically moves from one hole to the next and makes the vocal cords unhappy.

So make sure that there's no ice in your glass of water, and if you really love tea or coffee and you can't live without it—no problem. You simply need to make sure that the drink's not very hot. But then we still have another problem—the caffeine.

Addicted to Caffeine

When caffeine enters your body, it starts to speed everything up. That seems great in the morning, when you're trying to open your eyes and face a long workday ahead, but not so great when you're clearing your throat all the time because of too much mucus. Though providing a bit of extra energy sounds good in theory, caffeine actually ends up

taking moisture out of the body. That makes the mucus (the phlegm) in your throat thicker and harder to sing with.

If you're really married to caffeinated coffee, tea, or soda, I might be persuaded to let you have one a day. After that, however, I strongly recommend your switching to decaf coffee or herb tea. But I'm sure you know what I'd rather you drink: H_2O.

Dairy Products

Cheese, milk, yogurt—it sounds like the beginning of a TV commercial for a dairy farmers association. You expect to see a bunch of happy cows talking about vacationing in California. Then suddenly the star of the commercial, Bessie, starts to sing "Home on the Range," and she chokes on her own saliva.

No matter how you slice that cheese pizza, it's going to give you more phlegm than you want, more than you need, and more than you can sing comfortably with.

Remember, *phlegm* can be good or bad. It all depends on the consistency. If it's thin and watery, you've got a winner. If it's thick and hard, you've got a problem. Singing with too much phlegm is like trying to carry gold bars out of Fort Knox. You know there's something good in there, but you just can't get it out.

✷ ✷ ✷ ✷ ✷ ✷ ✷ ✷ ✷ ✷ ✷ ✷ ✷ ✷ ✷ ✷ ✷ ✷ ✷ ✷

Celebrity Tidbit

I asked superstar **Luther Vandross** about consuming dairy food, and here's what he said:

It's important not to have dairy products. They are mucus forming, and when there's phlegm, your singing is compromised.

I couldn't agree with Luther more. He talks about phlegm compromising your voice, and once the phlegm gets in there and clouds everything up, you just can't sing 100 percent anymore.

✷ ✷ ✷ ✷ ✷ ✷ ✷ ✷ ✷ ✷ ✷ ✷ ✷ ✷ ✷ ✷ ✷ ✷ ✷ ✷

So why do so many singers keep eating dairy? Maybe it's because it tastes so good, or because it's a big part of our history and culture. We're milk drinkers from birth, then we move from Mommy to the bottle, and a cow becomes our new best friend. Within a short period of time we're buttering our toast and placing it on the plate right next to a bowl with cereal and milk.

Some people can have a big-wheel pizza and wash it down with a sixteen-ounce glass of milk, and they still don't get any thick phlegm problems. If you're one of those people, more power to you. But if you're like most of us, and you're sick and tired of always clearing your throat when you try to sing, you need to cut back on the dairy products. It's not like they're so good for you anyway. There are plenty of better ways to get calcium. Eat broccoli, for example.

Alcohol

"Alcohol dehydrates the body." Have you ever heard that phrase? Do you know what it means? Just in case you're not 100 percent sure, let me explain. Alcohol gets into your system and basically pulls water out. That's hard on the vocal cords, because they need all the water they can get. As we learned earlier, the cords are at the back of the line when the body is handing out water. The last thing they need is for you to drink something that soaks up any of that water. But that's what alcohol does.

In classic movies you sometimes see Frank Sinatra, or Dean Martin, or Bing Crosby having an alcoholic drink before they go out on stage to sing. Sometimes you even see them on stage holding the drink. Many famous sings over the years have sworn by a glass or two of alcohol before they go on. Is there any scientific evidence that would support that kind of behavior? Unfortunately, there is. With your first one or two drinks, the alcohol actually lowers your anxiety, and is also a little bit stimulating. Most people have trouble focusing when they get anxious, so they sometimes feel that a drink calms their anxiety down, which helps them to focus better and to be more alert.

However, the bad news is, as soon as the alcohol stimulates you, it starts to put you to sleep, just like a sedative. The muscles in your body start to slow down and function less effectively.

Singing, even when you do it right, is hard work. You're going to need all of the power, stamina, and help your body can give you. Singing and alcohol are not a good mix. Any positive effects from the alcohol are so short-lived that they hardly count at all. And the negative ones last long enough to screw up your singing performance.

The choice is yours. But as long you have about four to six hours for your body to break down the alcohol before you sing, and you're not an alcoholic or pregnant, a couple of glasses of wine a day, or a couple of beers, is most probably fine.

Citrus

Remember the tea with honey and lemon your mother gave you? Well, so far we've learned that the water was too hot and the caffeine was a problem. Now what about the lemon? I'm sorry to say it, but I'd like you to lose that too. When you introduce citrus into your mouth it makes you salivate, and even though it might not make the phlegm that much thicker, any extra saliva, even the watery kind, can be a pain in the neck. Many people think that citrus cuts the phlegm, but over the last twenty-five years, I've seen just the opposite effect.

Sugar

There are plenty of vocal coaches and doctors who believe that you should limit your consumption of sugar on days when you need to sing. For a lot of people, extra sugar makes too much thick phlegm. Even if you're drinking lots of water to balance it out, it's still a good idea to cut back on the sugar thing.

✳ ✳ ✳ ✳ ✳ ✳ ✳ ✳ ✳ ✳ ✳ ✳ ✳ ✳ ✳ ✳ ✳ ✳ ✳

Celebrity Tidbit

cher

I asked superstar **Cher** about sugar, and here's what she said:

No chocolate before singing.

I think it's definitely good advice. It's a much better idea to sing your heart out during a performance, and then have some chocolate afterward as a reward for a job well done.

✳ ✳ ✳ ✳ ✳ ✳ ✳ ✳ ✳ ✳ ✳ ✳ ✳ ✳ ✳ ✳ ✳ ✳ ✳

Smoking

Let me tell you what smoking does to the vocal cords. After I do, I hope that you'll decide to be a professional singer instead of a professional smoker. Remember that there are two holes in the throat—one for food and liquid, and one for air—and that the vocal cords live down the air hole. Because of that, when you inhale anything—cigarettes, cigars, pot—the smoke goes straight to the vocal cords. Take a drag and a hot, chemical-filled cloud begins to dry up all the natural moisture you've worked so hard to get by drinking so much water.

No amount of smoking is healthy for the vocal cords. If you smoke and want to be a great singer, you need to stop. I do realize, however, that most smokers would love to stop, and that it's obviously not an easy thing to do. But in my heart of hearts, I believe that singing and smoking are opposite functions, and if you want to sing well, you have to find a way to make the change and quit.

Lots of smokers point to Frank Sinatra as an example of a person who could light up the stage while he kept lighting up, but I can guarantee that if Frank had quit, he would've had a hundred times more voice later on in life than he wound up with. You say he was good? I say he could've been a lot better. Incidentally, Sammy Davis Jr. died of throat cancer, which was directly related to his smoking.

The key point is that anything smoked (not salmon, of course), whether cigarettes, cigars, or pot, directly irritates the vocal cords with heat and chemicals. It also damages the lungs and eventually decreases the amount of air available for singing.

Chewing Gum

People come into my office all the time chewing gum. I've even seen singers who chew gum on stage during a performance. To illustrate why I always show them the wastebasket, let me ask you a couple of questions.

Do you notice that when you unwrap a new piece of gum it's completely dry?

Do you notice that if you were to chew that gum for a while and then take it out of your mouth, it would be completely dry again within seconds?

What does that tell you about the gum?

The answer is: The gum has no natural moisture in it. It uses all of your saliva to

keep it from drying out. And by the way, you don't have a lot of extra saliva to spare. You need all of it to help keep your throat moist and to sing better. So, you guessed it, I'm totally against chewing gum anytime near a performance. If you want to have gum after breakfast, fine, but after that I really don't recommend it.

Celebrity Tidbit

I asked superstar **Brian McKnight** if he followed any specific diet, and if he eats anything in particular before a performance, and here's what he said:

Actually, I eat whatever I want and don't really follow a specific diet for my voice. Before I sing, I really don't eat or drink anything. I believe singing well has to do with your confidence. Confidence triumphs over all!

A lot of singers don't eat anything before they sing. Digesting food can use up a lot of the body's energy, especially if you eat meat or anything else that the body has to work extra hard to digest. Just be selective and you'll be fine.

What About Lozenges and Throat Sprays?

I don't think you need them. What your vocal cords really need is water, and they're not getting it from these products. When you suck on a lozenge, the only real benefit comes from swallowing. Swallowing actually helps to lubricate the cords, so drinking water is a better solution because there's more swallowing going on. A lot of these products also make your throat numb, which I'm usually against. How can you sing if you can't feel the inside of your throat? **If your throat is sore when you swallow, you shouldn't sing that day at all.** If you actually do have pain, these products won't fix it anyway, they'll just mask it.

When you see throat sprays made especially for singers, keep in mind that they're mostly just water, with additives like eucalyptus. I've got nothing against eucalyptus, but the real effect of the spray comes from the water you *inhale*. It certainly wouldn't do you any good to just drink a concoction like this.

Recap

If you're drinking tons of water, cutting way back on the dairy intake, not smoking, not drinking a lot of citrus, and breathing in through your nose, you're going to enjoy much better vocal health. Your vocal cords are going to be happy and you're going to sing a lot better. What you eat does affect how you sing, so work with your body to make sure that the cords are always hydrated.

As I mentioned earlier, everyone is different and can therefore tolerate different foods. To see whether a food is hurting your voice, cut out one thing at a time. For example, stop drinking milk for about ten days and see if you're clearing your throat a lot less. It usually takes at least ten days to see if the body likes the change. Then, if you feel a lot better and you have a lot less thick phlegm in your throat, you can see that you're better off without the dairy. Next, stop drinking caffeinated soda for ten days and see how you sound and feel. One by one you can test what your body needs and doesn't need. At the end of a few weeks you'll have a diet that works for your voice. Try it out and see what happens.

BODY MOVEMENT

chapter NINE

Don't know what to do with your hands? Or your feet? No problem. I'll show you how to look like you're totally comfortable in your living room or on a big stage. We'll lose all of the moves that make you look silly, and replace them with things that make you shine.

The goal here is to make you feel and look comfortable in your own skin. If one of your legs is six inches shorter than the other, and you have the funniest haircut in town, but you walk out on stage with confidence and conviction, and you sing like a god or a goddess, after a few minutes the audience will forget all about your short leg and your funny haircut. They'll only be paying attention to the beautiful music coming out of your mouth.

When you listen to Celine Dion, do you stay focused on her awkward French pronunciation of English words, or do you simply lose yourself in the music and the incredible singing?

When Kid Rock is singing on stage, are you wasting your time focusing on all of his tattoos? Of course not. When he sings, the marks on his arms are the last thing on your mind.

When Christina Aguilera sings, are you so busy thinking about her tongue piercing that you can't focus on her singing? No way.

If you're the performer, a general rule is: **Whatever you focus on, so will the audience.** If your haircut is bothering you, and you keep playing with it, the audience will be thinking, Her hair is bugging her, and now it's bugging me.

Stage movement is about making sure that every move you make looks believable and natural. If you're the kind of person who waves his hands in big gestures when you speak to someone in a normal conversation, you can do the same thing when you're singing—as long as we make sure that it looks natural.

To accomplish that task, I want to first tell you my feelings about . . .

Parallel Gestures

As you may know, the left side of the brain controls the right side of the body, and vice versa, the right side of the brain controls the left side of the body. So when you raise your right hand and point your finger at someone, your left brain is making that happen.

Based on that truth, both sides of the body hardly ever do the exact same thing. So why is it that when you sing in front of people you start making gestures where both hands and arms are doing exactly the same thing at the same time?

Have you ever been to a kindergarten musical where all of the cute little kids are making the same specific moves while they sing? As precious as they are, I know you don't want to look like that.

Parallel gestures make you look uncomfortable, predictable, and unnatural. It makes people focus on your hands instead of on your singing and overall performance. Even though most of the population is guilty of this, including the President of the United States when he makes a speech on TV, parallel gestures are making you and him look less believable.

Mirror, Mirror on the Wall

I think this would be the perfect time to try a little test.

Go somewhere in your house where you have a nice big mirror on the wall. Now start to sing one of your favorite songs and pretend that you have an audience. As you sing and perform the song, I want you to go ahead and purposely make a lot of hand gestures. Let yourself go free and get into the song. Once you're really into the song, try to pay attention to what your hands are doing. Do you notice yourself making parallel gestures—both hands doing the same thing at the same time?

If you find your hands and arms doing a lot of the same thing, don't worry about it, I'll show you a way to make that disappear.

Remember that when you speak to someone on the street, in school, or at the coffee spot, when you use your hands you're not making parallel gestures—I guarantee it. So I'm not really asking you to learn anything new here. I'm simply asking you to do on stage what you do off stage. Be natural.

Practice singing songs in front of a mirror, and when you catch both hands doing the same thing, simply let one of the hands move to a slightly higher or lower position. Even changing it a tiny bit fixes the problem. I'm not saying, for example, that one hand has to be in front of you and the other has to be somewhere in China. The smallest difference is enough to make it look more natural.

Practice this mirror exercise until you get used to not doing the parallel gestures. Now that you know what not to do, you're mostly cured already.

Celebrity Tidbit

I asked superstar **Brian McKnight** if there was one piece of advice he would offer to someone who wants to be a singer, and here's what he said:

Concentrate on being the next you, not somebody else.

This book is all about finding the star in *you*. As long as you stay focused on being the best you can be, you'll end up a winner.

What About Your Eyes?

A singer is always trying to communicate on a totally real, honest level with his or her audience. The greatest singers I've ever heard made me feel as though they were singing to me alone—even in a room full of people. In fact, they made almost everyone feel as though they were part of an intimate exchange. How do they do that? The secret is brief eye contact.

If I was singing to you and staring right into your eyes the whole time, after about eight or ten seconds you'd start to feel uncomfortable, like we were two dogs in a stare-down, ready to fight for the same bone. When someone's staring at you, it's easy to feel challenged or threatened. But *brief eye contact* can have a completely different effect on your listeners. It can energize them and make them feel a real connection with you, and that's what makes them scream, cry, shout, and give you a standing ovation when you're finished singing.

If you're in a one-on-one situation, I suggest you use a technique I call the . . .

8-to-2 Ratio

Look at the person you're singing to and connect for about eight seconds, then look down slightly, as if you were thinking or looking inside of yourself for a moment. Then look right back at them for another eight seconds or so, and then look down again. Are you with me?

Make sure that you're not looking to the left or right of the person when you look away for your two seconds. When you do that, it makes the person think that there's something going on behind them to the left or right. It makes them want to turn back and see what you're looking at.

The *8-to-2 Ratio* is great for one-on-one, when you're singing to someone who's about five feet away from you. But if you're singing to a larger group of people, the rules change to what I call the . . .

Four-Second Shift

When you're on stage and you start to sing, go ahead and mentally divide the audience up into three sections:

* ✶ The center of the audience.
* ✶ The right side of the audience.
* ✶ The left side of the audience.

As you sing, I want you to divide your eye contact time in the following way:

* ✶ **Look at the center of the audience two-thirds of the time, which is a lot.**

✱ **Look at the right and left side of the audience the rest of the time, which is not that much!**

When you're making eye contact with one section, make direct eye contact with one person in that section. Hold the contact for about four seconds, and then make eye contact with someone else right next to that person. Keep going from person to person for about four seconds each, until you decide to move your focus to another section of the room.

Talk to the Head

A lot of singers just don't like looking into people's eyes—it makes them too nervous. If you're one of those singers, let me give you a technique that'll help you fool the audience into thinking that you're actually looking in their eyes anyway. It's a little technique I call *Talk to the Head.*

If I was about ten feet away from you and looking at your forehead, you would think that I was looking at your eyes. If I was looking at the hair on your head, you would still think that I was looking at your eyes. And, if I was looking at your chin, you would still think that I was looking at your eyes.

If you don't believe me, try it out for yourself. Get a friend to stand about ten feet away from you and tell them that you're going to be looking at their eyes, then do the following:

1. Look in their eyes and ask, "Am I looking at you?" and see what they say.
2. Look at their forehead and ask, "Am I looking at you?" and see what they say.
3. Look at their chin and ask, "Am I looking at you?" and see what they say.
4. Look at the hair on their head and ask, "Am I looking at you?" and see what they say.

I'll bet your friend will think you were looking at them the whole time. So until you feel comfortable looking right at people, feel free to simply look at their foreheads, and their looking back at you will have no chance of distracting you or making you feel nervous.

Stage Movement?

So many times when I go to see a performer, they're running all around the stage like an ice cube trapped in a blender. Instead of being exciting, the wild and meaningless movements are just making the audience seasick. Being a great performer is not about wasting your energy. It's about using your power to influence the audience. It's about making them cry, or smile, or dance, or sing along. It's about making them love you, respect you, want to spend more time with you, and rush out to the store and lay out $15 bucks for your latest CD. How you move on stage can either make you appealing or repelling, but the good news is, basic stage movement is really pretty simple. It all comes down to where, when, and how you move.

Where You Move

Learning *where* to move is as easy as following a simple pattern, and when you get it, you can sing in front of any audience anywhere. It's fine for an arena, the amphitheater, the local coffee shop, or just for standing on top of your bed. Learn my easy pattern just like a map, and it'll guide you through any performance.

Stage Movement

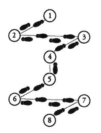

Point 1: This position, near the center of the stage, gives the audience its first chance to see and hear you.

Point 2: Walk toward the right and focus your attention on the audience sitting on that side. You'll only be turning your body slightly, so people sitting in the center and on the left side will still see plenty of your face.

Point 3: Change direction and walk toward the left side of the stage. Again, make sure that everyone in the room can still see a part of your face.

Point 4: Move back to center stage. You're now directly aligned with Point One, but you're closer to the audience.

Point 5: Most songs will end here, directly in line with Points 1 and 4, but a little closer to the crowd. This is the power position where you own the stage. You've conquered the back, the left, the right, and the front.

Points 6 through 8: Some songs are just longer, so they require more movement. If you've gotten all the way to Point Five and you've still got more song to go, move on to Point 6, a slight move to the right. From there, Point 7 moves you to the left side. And Point 8 brings you back to center for the end of the song.

Does this seem too simple? Good, it's supposed to be—and yet just about every performer you ever saw on stage was doing something like it. When you go to a concert and see Bruce Springsteen run to one side of the stage and jump up on a gigantic speaker to play and sing, he's at Point 2. As he runs to the other side of the stage and throws himself out into the audience, he's at Point 3.

This plan will still work even if there's almost no space at all to move. If you're performing in a space the size of a dinner plate, and you can't even take a single step, you can still go through all of the points above by moving your head in the right directions, or shifting your body one way or the other.

When to Move

How do you know *when* to move from point to point?

The answer is, if you learn to listen and use a bit of imagination, the music will tell you when it's time to move to change position.

Every song has a story to tell. Like scenes in a good movie, it moves in and out of a number of places and emotions. You have to become sensitive to where the changes are. One way to do this is by studying the lyrics.

Before you sing a song, print out the lyrics on a piece of paper and get ready to make some notes with a pencil. Look at the words and start to understand the story. For example, let's say that it's a love song. The story might go something like this:

Scene 1: In the beginning, the lyric might talk about how and when the lovers met.

Scene 2: Then it might talk about things they did, places they went, and feelings they shared.

Scene 3: Then maybe something bad happened to break the lovers apart.

Scene 4: Then they got back together, worked through all of their problems, and lived happily ever after.

Every good song has a story, and all stories can be broken up into separate and different parts. Those parts are what we use to decide when we move.

Also, remember that a song has music and melody. That really makes it easier to find the changes. In my imaginary love song example above, I'm sure that the music would change when the story does.

Scene 1: In the beginning, when the lyrics talk about how and when the lovers met, the music might be sweet and gentle.

Scene 2: Then when it spoke about the things the lovers did, places they went, and the feelings they shared, the music would probably get more intense and exciting.

Scene 3: When something bad happened to break the lovers apart, the music might change to be angrier, sadder, and painful, perhaps to a minor key.

Scene 4: Then when they've gotten back together, worked through all of their problems, and lived happily ever after, the music would most probably be joyful, happy, lively, and beautiful.

You can go over songs in the same way I just did. Doing so, you should easily find the places where the song changes mood, emotion, attitude, and story line. You should practice moving from point to point when those changes happen.

Doing this in front of a mirror or videotaping yourself will also help. That way you can become the audience as well, and see if the movement works or not. Just play around with all this and have fun.

How You Move

Now that I've given you some ideas to help you decide where and when to move, I need to give you some basic ideas about *how* to move.

The moment you step up to the mike, it's important to establish a strong presence and take control of the room.

How do you do that? By learning to stand still, at least for the first few seconds.

It's very important that the audience can easily see you in the first minute of your song. Whatever movements you make, you need to take that into consideration. If they can't focus on you, they won't even pay attention to you. Even if you're singing an up-tempo dance tune, you can remain relatively stationary at the very beginning of the song, containing yourself to one small area. You can move your body to the rhythm, but try to keep your feet near the same place. The goal here is to let the audience make a few of the following decisions about you:

* **Do they like what you are wearing?**
* **Do they know the song?**
* **Do they like the song?**
* **Do they like your voice?**

Believe it or not, the audience starts making all kinds of judgments about you right at the beginning of your performance. You'd think they could at least wait until you've sung a song or two before they decide whether they like you, but that's just not the way it normally goes. You've heard the expression "Time is money," right? Well, even though the audience is often wrong, they decide really fast whether or not they're going to give you any more of their valuable time and attention. So you need to make sure to win them over in the first minute. Once that happens, they'll cut you some slack, and give you a lot more time to showcase your talents. So make sure that in the very beginning of your song you don't jump all around the stage with your arms flailing.

Also, you don't have to be a dance queen at the same time you're a singing diva. When Janet Jackson, Jennifer Lopez, or Britney Spears sings and dances, they're not always singing. Sorry to burst your bubble, but when the dancing gets rough, the singers usually just pretend to sing, and the actual vocal the audience hears is on tape. You probably don't have your own soundman and the option of lip-synching, so only dance as much as you can without sacrificing the singing. Save enough energy to make beautiful music come out of your mouth.

YOUR
DAILY
WARM-UP

chapter
TEN

On the accompanying CD I've given you a special set of vocal warm-ups to help make your voice grow to its maximum potential. Every day you sing along with them, you'll feel your voice getting stronger, more powerful, and more beautiful. In no time flat you'll be amazed at the things your new voice can do.

I want to explain a bit about how and why the exercises are designed the way they are. It comes down to the following things:

How to Make the Instrument Strong

If you wanted to have the perfect body, one of the things you might choose to do is to go to the gym regularly. You could put together a series of exercises that would get different parts of your body in shape. You might use weights to get bigger arm muscles, the treadmill to get a good cardio workout, sit-ups for your abs, and so on. After a while, you and hopefully all of the people who see you would notice the positive changes. Friends might even be standing in line around the pool just to touch your new beautiful stomach.

When you work on your physical body, the changes are on the outside for people to see. It's totally different with the voice. You can't see the vocal cords, so how do you know that the exercises you're doing are making them stronger?

Some people think that the vocal cords respond like your bicep muscles do. You lift weights and break the muscles down, then they come back stronger and bigger. Those people, however, know nothing at all about the voice. Please let me explain . . .

When you overuse the voice, the vocal cords get red and swollen. From that point on, all your cords are trying to do is to get back to the condition they were in before you abused them. They don't come back stronger. Quite the contrary, every time you make them puffy and swollen, they become weaker, and in the long run they get more fragile.

The exercises I'm giving you on the CD are designed to make sure that you never hurt the cords. Each exercise is designed to make the vocal cords move to the perfect place to find chest, middle, and head voice. Every day that you do them, you're learning how to better operate the machinery that you own. That's what a great technique is all about. If you have a $100,000 piano in your living room and all you can play is "Chopsticks," you're not making the most out of your instrument. My exercises will give you the strength to create the sounds you need. No matter how difficult the song you choose to sing is, your voice will be healthy, happy, and ready for the challenge.

How to Get Control Over the Amount of Air

The CD exercises start out with sounds like *goog* and *gug*, and then move toward *mum, no, nay,* and *nah.* That progression is designed to control exactly how much air gets to the vocal cords. Let me explain . . .

Go ahead and say the word *gug.* The *G* at the front and the *G* at the end actually stop the air for a split second. That's what I want. My exercise program starts out by having you produce tiny bursts of air, and then little by little as you warm up, the exercises have you keep sending more and more air to the cords. By the end of the warmup, you have lots of air coming to really thick and strong vocal cords.

If you were a dancer getting ready to perform, you would most probably want to do some stretching. It would be pretty silly for you to start by jumping high into the air and landing on the ground doing splits. That might postpone the performance . . . at least until you got back from the hospital.

Just so, more and more air gradually comes to the cords and you get used to dealing with it. In about fifteen to twenty minutes you'll feel powerful enough to open your mouth and sing to your adoring fans, your cat, or just sing for your supper.

Celebrity Tidbit

I asked superstar **Luther Vandross** how he warms up his voice before a performance, and here's what he said:

Vocal silence for the hours before the performance is very helpful. Also, warm drinks (tea, water, etc.) will work. Doing scales on the vowel sound ooo *helps, too.*

Great advice. A lot of singers try to stay silent for a little while before the gig. Celine Dion is famous for not speaking most of the day. Luther also reinforces our belief in never drinking anything too hot, and tells us that his favorite singing exercise is with the *ooo* sound. That goes along great with the GOOG exercise I've already given you.

How to Deal with Vowels and Consonants

Different vowels and consonants make the shape of your mouth and the back part of your throat change its size. That's why when you're singing a song, some words are easy to sing and some are not. Some words just roll right off the tip of your tongue, and some just seem to get stuck in the back part of your throat. To help you understand why, I want to explain the difference between open and closed vowels.

If you were to say *"Eeeeeeee,"* the back part of your throat would be fairly closed, and your upper and lower teeth would be close to one another. Because of the closed throat and the small mouth position, this sound is called a *closed vowel.*

Try saying the following sounds all strung together, holding out each sound for a couple of seconds: *e-oo-oh-ah.* Do it again and concentrate on the back part of your

throat: *e-oo-oh-ah*. Do you feel how your throat starts out kind of closed and then opens up a little bit more with each different sound? The *ah* is called an *open vowel,* and when you say *e-oo-oh-ah,* you're going from closed vowels to open ones. Get it?

The warm-ups are specifically designed so that you go from closed vowels to open ones. That way the cords don't freak out by having a huge amount of air come through a big open throat and blow them out of the way. Each little *goog* and *gug* opens up the throat just a little bit more, so that by the end of the warm-up you can handle just about anything.

How to Go from Doing the Warm-Ups to Actually Singing Songs

When you first learn any new vocal technique, including mine, it's important to concentrate on the warm-up exercises. They're specially designed to make it as easy on you as possible. Most techniques have been around in one form or another for hundreds of years. Great vocal warm-up exercises really do make your voice stronger, thicker, and higher, as well as give you power and control.

That's all fine and dandy in the beginning, but what happens when you master the exercises and you try to sing songs?

Is there any guarantee that your voice will suddenly burst out like Whitney, Mariah, or Christina?

Do good warm-ups always mean great singing? Not always.

Great singing happens when the right amount of air meets the right amount of cord (one of my favorite lines). Remember, the warm-ups are designed to control exactly what the air and cords are doing. *Songs are not.*

Believe me, the songwriter's not thinking about *your* voice when he writes the song. He's trying to create the perfect melody and lyric. Whether or not somebody can sing it is the furthest thing from his mind. He's not crafting the vowels and consonants for singing; he's creating a work of art.

So, quite often when singers move from doing the warm-ups to doing the songs, they get into trouble. In order to make things easier, try the following ideas:

Flip-Flopping

If you're so good with *mum* or *nay,* why don't we use it? Take your best sound from the warm-ups and sing the song with that instead of with the real words. "Somewhere Over the Rainbow" would be *"mum-mum, mum-mum-mum-mum-mum.* When you try these sounds as a song, you'll notice that it's suddenly easier to hit all of the notes. The warm-up sounds make just about any song a whole lot easier to sing.

Now, I want you to start *flip-flopping;* by that I mean go back and forth between the warm-up sounds and the actual words. Try it bit by bit. Sing a small part of the song with, for example, *mum,* then go right back and sing the same small part with the words. The goal here is to make both times feel the same.

This technique is extremely useful on the really hard parts of the song, usually the high notes. Play around with it and you'll see how well it works.

Make a Road Map

If you're learning a new song and you actually have the sheet music, you can look and see where the chest, middle, and head voice notes are. By the way, you don't have to know how to read music to do this. It's really easy. Let me show you.

If you look at the above illustrations, one for male and the other for female, you'll see that I've marked off where chest, middle, and head actually live on the musical staff. You can easily go through sheet music when you get it and make a little mark by the notes that cross over into the middle area. For example, if a woman was looking at a piece of music and saw a note that was on the third line of the staff, which is a B, she would know to go into middle voice. If the note went lower than the third line, she would know to come back to her chest voice.

Do you get it?

This method should really help you while you're learning how to go from warm-ups to songs.

Once you have a killer middle voice, you won't need to work this hard. When your chest, middle, and head voices are all connected and working together, you should be able to sing songs and have the voice just go wherever it's supposed to go, without a lot of mental planning. Until then, use all of these tricks to help you out.

Can I Warm Up by Singing Songs?

A lot of singers think that singing their songs over and over before a show will warm up their voices, but that's not usually the case. If there's any straining or pressure happening when you sing the songs, you're not warming up, you're wearing down your voice.

Runners don't warm up by running the race right before the race. They stretch.

Dancers don't warm up by dancing before the performance. They stretch.

Singers should do exactly the same thing: Stretch before singing. To do that, you need to practice the warm-up exercises.

How Often Should I Practice?

I would love for you to practice at least five days a week for a minimum of ten to fifteen minutes. Both the male and female warm-ups on the CD fit into that time frame. Practice in the car on your way to school or work, or at home on the weekends. Try to make a regular schedule that you keep to. By making it a set time on specific days, you'll have a better chance of keeping it up.

Also, make sure that you always practice before you sing songs. Don't even think about getting up at the local karaoke bar or café and belting out a tune if you haven't done your warm-ups that day. If you're really pressed for time, even five to ten minutes will help a lot.

Warming up is not only about making you sound better, which it does, it's about making sure that your voice stays healthy. A runner who doesn't stretch has a much greater chance of pulling a muscle. A singer who doesn't stretch by doing the warm-ups has just as much chance to hurt themselves.

If you've ever been backstage at a concert, you would have most probably heard the singer going through scales trying to warm up. It's not because they like doing the exercises so much, it's more of a necessity to keep the show on the road. No singer, no tour; no tour, no money. Practicing for a few minutes a day is a small price to pay for always being able to count on your voice.

Celebrity Tidbit

brian McKNIGHT

I asked superstar **Brian McKnight** what was the funniest thing that ever happened to him while he was singing, and here's what he said:

Twice when I was performing I fell off the stage.

Oops.

Who Should Practice What

When boys and girls are growing up, they start out with voices that are very similar. They share the same basic singing range. They start down low together, and hit just about the same ceiling on the top. They even go from chest to middle to head voice in the same exact places. But all of that drastically changes when a young man reaches puberty. At that point, a boy's voice drops a whole octave (about twelve notes) and picks up a totally new bassy, thick, lower-sounding voice. Along with that change comes the fact that the chest, middle, and head voice are all in different spots too. All of the transitions and seams you got used to before are now in different places. That's why most boys never sing high again after their voices change. Being a boy soprano one day and a bass or baritone the next can be a bit of a shock to the body and the voice. My students, however, never lose their highs. As long as they keep working on chest, middle, and head, they get used to the new lower sounds, and just add that bottom to the top they already have. **So with regard to all the warm-up exercises on the CD:**

1. **All women, no matter how young or old, should practice using the female exercises on the CD.**
2. **If you're a young man whose voice hasn't changed yet, you should practice using the female exercises on the CD.**
3. **Men whose voices have already changed should use the male exercises on the CD.**

Do You Have What It Takes?

In the privacy of your own home, you sing and dance and jump around like a seasoned superstar. One day you see an advertisement for an audition. Somebody somewhere is looking for something to be sung. You reach down to pick up the phone but your fingers cramp up. You think to yourself, Do I really have what it takes? Am I ready to be a professional singer? What if I'm not as good as I think I am?

First, let me say that every professional singer I've ever met had plenty of days when they felt exactly the same way. Even the greatest singers in the world have times when they question their own abilities; it's only human. No matter how much ego you might have, singing is a humbling experience. It's hard to always sound great. You get ready to sing, open your mouth, and hope that wonderful sounds will come out, but sometimes that just doesn't happen. There are so many things that can affect the way you sing. One minute you could sound like an angel, and the next like a drowning duck. At best, the voice is always a little bit unpredictable. That's why singing is sometimes a tough gig. It's easy to wonder if you've got what it takes, especially if the voice changes from day to day.

So many different things affect your singing. That's why I usually say that voice is the most difficult instrument in the world. Think about it. If you own a piano and you tune it every six months or so, that piano will be exactly the same every time you open the lid and start to play it. Even if there was a huge earthquake and the house fell down on top of it, once you got past the rubble, the piano would still probably be just fine. The voice, however, is not that lucky. There are thousands of things that can easily affect your voice. Here are just a few:

1. **What you eat or drink:** We've covered most of that in the chapter on diet.
2. **What kind of mood you're in:** It's hard to sing when you're in a bad mood,

or tired, or angry, or frustrated. Your emotions play a big role when it comes to singing. How you feel at that moment can make it harder or easier on your body and your voice.

3. **Air-conditioning or heating:** Earlier we learned that the best way to keep your voice healthy is to keep the vocal cords hydrated, that is, full of water. So you never want to do things that make them get dry. Well, heating and air-conditioning units suck all of the moisture out of the air. When you spend a lot of time breathing dry air, it makes you sound bad.

4. **Your menstrual cycle:** During the menstrual cycle there's less blood flow to the vocal cords. That makes it harder to sing.

5. **The weather:** Hot, cold, humid, rainy, and snowy conditions all affect the voice, because they affect the body in general. For example, if it's hot or humid you sweat more, and when you sweat more you become dehydrated and also get thick phlegm. Thick phlegm makes it harder to sing well. The weather can also affect your allergies, which can easily ruin a good day of singing.

6. **Your warm-up routine:** By practicing the daily warm-up exercises, you have a much better chance of sounding great every day. Even though the voice may change on a regular basis, the exercises level everything out. On days that you feel weak and in bad voice, you can practice the exercises for a longer time. On days that you feel terrific, you can just do a shorter warm-up. By adjusting the amount of time you spend exercising, you can compensate for however you feel that day. The warm-ups are the medicine: You decide how big of a dose you need that day to fix the problem.

✳ ✳ ✳ ✳ ✳ ✳ ✳ ✳ ✳ ✳ ✳ ✳ ✳ ✳ ✳ ✳ ✳ ✳ ✳ ✳

Celebrity Tidbit

luther VANDROSS

I asked superstar **Luther Vandross** if there was one piece of advice he would offer to someone who wants to be a singer, and here's what he said:

You have to confront yourself with these questions:

1. *Do I really have what it takes?*
2. *Can I weather the rejections that will inevitably come?*

In the end, it's all about working hard to achieve an incredibly rewarding goal. Being a singer is an amazing accomplishment, and one of the greatest jobs in the world. So "having what it takes" is about doing whatever you need to do to become the best. Will there be obstacles? Of course, millions of them, just like Luther says. But if you're willing to deal with the rejections and the hardships, and still work hard every day to accomplish your goals, *anything is possible!*

✷ ✷ ✷ ✷ ✷ ✷ ✷ ✷ ✷ ✷ ✷ ✷ ✷ ✷ ✷ ✷ ✷ ✷ ✷

Let's Warm Up

Here's a list of the warm-up exercises on the CD. I would love it if you practiced them regularly. A good amount would be three to five times per week, though I would love it if you practiced even more than that. Remember, though, I only want you to do the full warm-up routine once a day. After the daily warm-up, feel free to sing songs all day and night if you want. *Just have fun.*

ONE-OCTAVE EXERCISE
Goog
Gug
Mum
No
Nay
Nah

OCTAVE-AND-HALF EXERCISE
Goog
Gug
Mum
No
Nay
Nah

ONE-OCTAVE JUMP
Gee
Gug
Mum

(ALL WOMEN, NO MATTER HOW YOUNG OR OLD,
AND YOUNG MEN WHOSE VOICES HAVEN'T CHANGED YET,
SHOULD GO TO TRACK 21 ON THE CD)

(MEN WHOSE VOICES HAVE ALREADY CHANGED
SHOULD GO TO TRACK 22 ON THE CD)

Till We Meet Again

I want to tell you how proud I am to be your teacher. I've thrown a ton of stuff at you throughout the book. I've asked you to make all kinds of funny sounds, and you've been a great sport. I hope you had fun along the way.

I know that if you've done all that I've asked, your singing has indeed improved dramatically. Just remember, singing is always a work in progress. The goal is to get better every day that you sing. If you love to perform as much as I do, you'll keep working on the exercises and continue growing.

You've come so far . . . I can't wait to hear you on stage, or buy your new record in the stores! Anything is possible if you believe in yourself enough, and work every day to overcome any obstacles that may appear.

Best of luck in the future, and I'll be listening for you . . .

Roger Love

Acknowledgments

Eiko, Jim, and Jacques Chatel. You are the best parents (and brother) a son-in-law could ever wish for. I love you very much.

Gayliann Harvey. I'm positive there was a mix-up at birth. Though it says "Harvey" on your birth certificate, you are truly a "Love." Also, thanks for creating the illustrations for the book.

Tabitha, Andie, Sam, and Tim De La Torre. It feels like we have known each other for many years. I will continue to treasure our friendship for at least a thousand more—best friends are hard to find.

Tina, Alexa, and Philip Love. Thanks for caring.

Scott Alberts. You are a wonderful friend and business partner. Thank you for your creativity, kindness, and insight.

Michael, Shaun, and Janine Alberts. Thank you for sharing Scott with me.

The Oakwood School. Thanks for looking out for our daughter . . . and her parents.

BJ Robbins. Thank you for your guidance, and your faith in me as a writer.

Lauren McKenna. Thank you for the opportunity to create something new, and for your help along the way.

Chrissy Swearingen (at Hal Leonard). Thank you for your help securing the lyric reprint rights. I couldn't have done it without you.

Yoshiki and Extasy Records. Thank you for your friendship, and for allowing me to be a part of the Extasy family.

Ana "Lupe" Marquez. Thank you for taking such good care of us.

Ilene Feldman and Koji Toyoda. It's an honor to be friends with both of you.

Anna, Grace, Tammy, and Kevin Leichter. I came over to borrow a cup of sugar, and ended up getting a whole plate of kindness and caring. Here's to our future together, and a lot more meals over at your house.

Tom Sturges and Antonina Armato. Thanks for the love and support.

Dr. Jay Gordon for always being there.

Thanks also to Willa, Scout, and Robyn Bennett; Linda, Maia, Aliah, and Russ Candioty-Werth; Vance, Jameson, Chynna, and William Baldwin; Alex, Maddy, and Ray Colcord; Peter D. Pergelides; The Harkavy's; Nikki Freeman; Chris Russo; Justin Smith; the Lanning's; Lynne and Terry Clinch; Megan McKeever; Tina Kennedy; Paolo and Azma Shab; the Selznick's; the Chabassier's; the Dole's; Kim Kimbro; the Munatones'; Jackie West-Cole.

A special thanks to my friends at Tigi-Bedhead.

Thanks to Luther Vandross; Cher; Nelly; Christina Aguilera; and Brian McKnight.

Copyright information for the Love Note songs:

Beautiful

Words and Music by Linda Perry
Copyright © 2002 by Famous Music Corporation and Stuck In The Throat Music
All Rights Administered by Famous Music Corporation
International Copyright Secured. All Rights Reserved.

Don't Know Why

Words and Music by Jesse Harris
Copyright © 2002 Sony/ATV Songs LLC and Beanly Songs
All Rights Administered by Sony/ATV Music Publishing,
8 Music Square West, Nashville, TN 37203
International Copyright Secured. All Rights Reserved.

U Got It Bad

Words and Music by Usher Raymond, Jermaine Dupri and Bryan Michael Cox
Copyright © 2000 EMI APRIL MUSIC INC., UR-IV MUSIC, SO SO DEF MUSIC,
BABYBOY'S LITTLE PUBLISHING CO. and NOONTIME SOUTH INC.
All Rights for UR-IV MUSIC and SO SO DEF MUSIC Controlled and Administered by EMI APRIL MUSIC INC.
All Rights Reserved. International Copyright Secured. Used by Permission.

Love Notes™

are protected under one or more of the following patents 6,546,229 B1
"Music Notes" chapter

AVAILABLE ON DVD AND HOME VIDEO

YOUR OWN PRIVATE VOICE LESSON WITH ROGER LOVE

Turn Your *Stage Fright* Into STAR QUALITY...
and *Get Ready for the Spotlight!*

MusicSpace•com   www.MusicSpace.com/lovetosing   *RAZOR & TIE*

Don't even pretend you won't read more.

The Whole
JOHN REED
It all began with a small boy and a large hole. Where will the whole thing end?

Generation S.L.U.T.
MARTY BECKERMAN
A brutal feel-up session with today's sex-crazed teens.

Lit Riffs
What happens when your favorite writers write stories inspired by your favorite songs? You're about to find out . . . includes riffs by: Tom Perrotta, Jonathan Lethem, Aimee Bender, Neal Pollack, Amanda Davis, JT LeRoy, Lisa Tucker, and many more!

Door to Door
TOBI TOBIN
She controls who does and doesn't get in. But when's she going to get in herself?

A Hip-Hop Story
HERU PTAH
Words become powerful weapons as two MCs fight to be #1.

The Perks of Being a Wallflower
STEPHEN CHBOSKY
Standing on the fringes offers a unique perspective on life. But sometimes you've got to see what it looks like from the dance floor.

More from the young, the hip, and the up-and-coming.
Brought to you by MTV Books

MTV: Music Television and MTV Books are trademarks of
MTV Networks, a Divison of Viacom International, Inc.

POCKET BOOKS
A Division of Simon & Schuster
A VIACOM COMPANY

11227

As many as 1 in 3 Americans
have HIV and don't know it.

TAKE CONTROL.
KNOW YOUR STATUS.
GET TESTED.

To learn more about HIV testing,
or get a free guide to HIV and
other sexually transmitted diseases.

www.knowhivaids.org
1-866-344-KNOW

09764